Six Poems by Joseph Smith

Six Poems by Joseph Smith

A Dimension of Meaning
in the Doctrine and Covenants

Colin B. Douglas

TEMPLE HILL BOOKS

ISBN 978-1-4341-0383-3

Copyright 2015 by Colin B. Douglas. All rights reserved.
Printed in the United States of America.

The views expressed in this book are the responsibility of the author and do not necessarily represent the position of the publisher. The reader alone is responsible for the use of any ideas or information provided by this book.

Published by Temple Hill Books, an imprint of The Editorium.

Temple Hill Books™, the Temple Hill Books logo, and The Editorium™ are trademarks of The Editorium, LLC.

The Editorium, LLC
West Jordan City, UT 84081-6132
templehillbooks.com
templehill@editorium.com

Contents

Introduction	1
Doctrine and Covenants 93	5
Doctrine and Covenants 76	37
Doctrine and Covenants 88:1–68	63
Doctrine and Covenants 1	77
Doctrine and Covenants 133	91
Doctrine and Covenants 121:1–25, 122:1–9	103
Further Observations and Some Conclusions	113
Works Cited	127

Introduction

My thesis is that these selections from the Doctrine and Covenants are impressive poems and that to be fully understood they must be read as such. That is, they mean *presentationally* as well as *discursively*, by "how they say" as well as by "what they say," by saying what they say in a particular way and a particular context. (For more explanation of the terms *presentational* and *discursive*, see Susanne K. Langer, *Philosophy in a New Key*, and Eliseo Vivas, *Creation and Discovery*.) Furthermore, in their full presentational nature, they achieve an aesthetic unity that qualifies them to be called poems. Though their didactic purposes cannot be ignored, I do not propose a mere "appreciation" of them as "literature" in addition to those extraliterary values. I do not mean that the so-called "literary" aspects of these works are merely "beautiful means of embellishment," the "casket" within which "the jewel of thought" is enclosed, as Orson F. Whitney might have described them (*The Poetical Writings of Orson F. Whitney*, pp. 5, 156). Rather, they are essential aspects of the thought; they are among the means by which the works "mean"; and to ignore them is to ignore a dimension of meaning. The explication of what are often considered "merely" aesthetic values is an essential component of a hermeneutic for works such as these; for Joseph Smith was a poet-prophet—a poet whose "matter" was his revelatory experiences, and a prophet who articulated—*constituted*—his experiences through the process of poetic creation. In him, the functions of poet and prophet are inseparable.

The commentaries that follow are elementary exercises in poetry explication, the extent of my ambition being to call attention to the fact that these texts reward a "literary" reading and merit closer attention by more adequate readers. The explications are cast in the language of an old critical creed, but it is, I trust, a creed not wholly outworn, and it is the one in which I was suckled. It seems suitable, indeed necessary, for elementary work on "the works of Joseph Smith" that should have been done and surpassed many years ago.

The best evidence for how all these works might have been composed and recorded is Parley P. Pratt's account in connection with section 129 (which is not included here):

> Each sentence was uttered slowly and very distinctly, and with a pause between each, sufficiently long for it to be recorded, by an ordinary writer, in longhand.
>
> This was the manner in which all his written revelations were dictated and written. There was never any hesitation, reviewing, or reading back, in order to keep the run of the subject; neither did any of these communications undergo revisions, underlinings, or corrections. As he dictated them so they stood, so far as I have witnessed (*Autobiography*, pp. 65–66).

I have endeavored to reflect the manner in which I surmise they might have been delivered by the manner in which I have set them forth typographically, in thought units. I also have broken them up as seems appropriate into parts and paragraphs (or stanzas, since we are speaking here of poetry). The line breaks indicate how the works might have been delivered and might be read, with a slight pause at each line break. Following the lead of Robert Alter in *The Art of Biblical Poetry*, I refer to the segments that begin flush left and continue indented as *lines*, and the smaller segments within those as *versets*.

I have preserved the exact wording of the current official edition of the Doctrine and Covenants, with exceptions contained in brackets and explained in the commentary. I am aware that these works have a textual history as they have passed through the hands of scribes and editors, but any variations are irrelevant to the present purpose. I have revised punctuation freely, however. The revisions I have made to punctuation are only what any attentive reader must do privately, if only mentally, in the process of explication; typographical arrangement and punctuation are, after all, tools of explication, even as exercised by the first editors, who for the most part were working with material that was dictated orally; and when something does not seem coherent the reader must supply, at least mentally, what seems to be implied in order to find a coherence. As to the few emendations to wording, I am aware that tinkering with the wording of sacred texts is serious business. In making these emendations I am not seeking to steady any arks by proposing changes in the canonized text. I have revised this language merely by way of attempted interpretation of sometimes difficult text.

Some readers might be troubled by my calling Joseph Smith the author of these works, for are they not the word of God, and is God therefore not the author? I submit that, for hermeneutical purposes, it is more helpful to understand some things about scripture by treating it as written not by God but by men in response to their experience with God. (This actually has been a principle of biblical hermeneutics since Friedrich Schleiermacher [1768–1834].) It is meaningless to speak of God's literary style or method, for God will employ any style or method that will accomplish his purpose; but when he speaks to men, in order to be understood by them, he must necessarily speak according to their understanding; and therefore, at least indirectly, the human mind through which revelation comes to the rest of us necessarily has a part in shaping it, even when (as I am inclined to think happens only exceptionally, though my own experience with revelation is admittedly limited) the words are dictated one by one. The words of Isaiah are in a different Hebrew style from that of the words of Amos, and that is best explained by differences in the minds of Isaiah and Amos, and perhaps of their audiences; and in section 1, which is called "the Lord's preface" to the Doctrine and Covenants, the Lord is presented as saying that the contents of the Doctrine and Covenants "were given unto [his] servants in their weakness, after the manner of their language, that they might come to understanding." I draw further support from this paragraph in *The Joseph Smith Papers: Revelations and Translations, Manuscript Revelation Books*, p. xxix:

> Joseph Smith and his followers considered his revelations to be true in the sense that they communicated the mind and will of God, not infallible in an idealized sense of literary flawlessness. "The revelations were not God's diction, dialect, or native language," historian Richard Bushman has written. "They were couched in language suitable to Joseph's time" (*Rough Stone Rolling*, p. 174). Smith and others appointed by revelation (including Oliver Cowdery, Sydney Rigdon, John Whitmer, and William W. Phelps) edited the revelations based on the same assumption that informed their original receipt: namely, that although Smith represented the voice of God, who was condescending to speak to him, he was limited by a "crooked broken scattered and imperfect language" (JS, Kirtland, Ohio, to William W. Phelps, [Independence, Missouri], 27 Nov. 1832, in JS Letterbook I, 4).

To appropriate and paraphrase from Ezra Pound (*The Spirit of Romance*, pp. 7–8), who was speaking of art, in particular literary art, the river of revelation is colored by the bed in which it runs, that bed being the human mind. That God has set his approval on a text as representing his mind and will (as through the process of canonization) is sufficient reason to call him ultimately the author of it; and a second reason is that he has given by revelation the "matter" of the text; but differences in style and other aspects of composition, and perhaps even of content, are better explained by calling a human being the author. It was no less a prophet (and poet, and explicator of texts) than Nephi, after all, who wrote of the greatness of "the words of Isaiah," not the greatness of the words of God as dictated to Isaiah. God can compose in any manner he chooses, and it will always be adequate to his purpose, but the choice of one manner or another is to be explained in terms of the needs and capabilities of human minds, the mind of the human "author" and the mind of the intended hearer or reader of the work. The words that follow "thus saith the Lord" (implied or explicit) are always the words as reported by a human being to human beings as a human being has received them, and the words are unavoidably conditioned by that human element. Moreover, this approach leaves more common ground on which to discuss these works with those of non–Latter-day-Saint faith or of no faith. Therefore, "six poems by Joseph Smith."

Doctrine and Covenants 93

i

NARRATOR:

¹Verily, thus saith the Lord:

THE LORD:

It shall come to pass that every soul
   who forsaketh his sins,
   and cometh unto me,
   and calleth on my name,
   and obeyeth my voice,
   and keepeth my commandments
shall see my face
   and know that I am,
²and that I am the true light
   that lighteth every man
   that cometh into the world,
³and that I am in the Father,
   and the Father in me,
and the Father and I are one—
⁴   the Father because he gave me of his fulness
   and the Son because I was in the world
   and made flesh my tabernacle
   and dwelt among the sons of men.
⁵I was in the world and received of my Father,
   and the works of him were plainly manifest.

⁶And John saw and bore record of the fulness of my glory,
   and the fulness of John's record is hereafter to be revealed;

⁷and he bore record, saying:

JOHN:

I saw his glory,
   that he was in the beginning
   before the world was.
⁸Therefore, in the beginning the Word was,
   for he was the Word,
   even the messenger of salvation,
⁹the light and the Redeemer of the world,
   the Spirit of truth,
   who came into the world,
because the world was made by him,
   and in him was the life of men
   and the light of men.
¹⁰The worlds were made by him;
   men were made by him;
all things were made by him,
   and through him,
   and of him.

¹¹And I, John, bear record

that I beheld his glory
   as the glory of the Only Begotten of the Father,
   full of grace and truth,
even the Spirit of truth,
   which came and dwelt in the flesh
   and dwelt among us.
¹²And I, John, saw that he received not of the fulness at the first
   but received grace for grace;
¹³and he received not of the fulness at first
   but continued from grace to grace
   until he received a fulness;
¹⁴and thus he was called the Son of God,
   because he received not of the fulness at the first.

¹⁵And I, John, bear record,

and lo, the heavens were opened,
   and the Holy Ghost descended upon him in the form of a dove
   and sat upon him,
and there came a voice out of heaven saying,
   "This is my beloved Son."

¹⁶And I, John, bear record

that he received a fulness of the glory of the Father;
¹⁷   and he received all power,
   both in heaven and on earth,
and the glory of the Father was with him,
   for he dwelt in him.

THE LORD:

¹⁸And it shall come to pass that,
   if you are faithful,
   you shall receive the fulness of the record of John.
¹⁹I give unto you these sayings
   that you may understand
   and know how to worship
   and know what you worship,
that you may come unto the Father in my name
   and in due time receive of his fulness;
²⁰for, if you keep my commandments,
   you shall receive of his fulness
   and be glorified in me as I am in the Father.
Therefore, I say unto you,
   you shall receive grace for grace.

ii

THE LORD:

²¹And now, verily I say unto you:

I was—in the beginning—with the Father,
   and am the Firstborn,
²²and all those who are begotten through me
   are partakers of the glory of the same
   and are the church of the Firstborn.

²³Ye were also—
  in the beginning,
  with the Father—
that which is Spirit,
  even the Spirit of truth;
²⁴and truth is knowledge of things as they are,
  and as they were,
  and as they are to come;
²⁵and whatsoever is more or less than this
  is the spirit of that wicked one
  who was a liar from the beginning.
²⁶The Spirit of truth is of God;
  I am the Spirit of truth;

and John bore record of me, saying:

JOHN:

He received a fulness of truth,
  yea, even of all truth;
²⁷and no man receiveth a fulness
  unless he keepeth his commandments.
²⁸He that keepeth his commandments receiveth truth and light
  until he is glorified in truth and knoweth all things.

THE LORD:

²⁹Man was also—
  in the beginning—
  with God;
intelligence,
  or the light of truth,
was not created or made,
  neither indeed can be.
³⁰All truth is independent in that sphere in which God has placed it,
  to act for itself,
as all intelligence also;
  otherwise there is no existence.
³¹Behold, here is the agency of man,
  and here is the condemnation of man,
because that which was from the beginning
  is plainly manifest unto them,
  and they receive not the light,

Doctrine and Covenants 93

³²and every man whose spirit receiveth not the light
   is under condemnation;
³³for man is spirit;
   the elements are eternal;
and spirit and element,
   inseparably connected,
   receive a fulness of joy;
³⁴and, when separated,
   man cannot receive a fulness of joy.
³⁵The elements are the tabernacle of God;
   yea, man is the tabernacle of God,
   even temples;
and whatsoever temple is defiled,
   God shall destroy that temple.
³⁶The glory of God is intelligence,
   or, in other words, light and truth;
³⁷ light and truth forsake that evil one.
³⁸Every spirit of man was innocent in the beginning,
   and, God having redeemed man from the fall,
   men became again, in their infant state, innocent before God;
³⁹and that wicked one cometh and taketh away light and truth,
   through disobedience,
   from the children of men,
   and because of the tradition of their fathers.

iii

THE LORD:

⁴⁰But I have commanded you
   to bring up your children in light and truth.

⁴¹But, verily, I say unto you, my servant Frederick G. Williams:

You have continued under this condemnation:
⁴² you have not taught your children light and truth,
   according to the commandments;
and that wicked one hath power, as yet, over you,
   and this is the cause of your affliction.

⁴³And now a commandment I give unto you:

If you will be delivered you shall set in order your own house,
    for there are many things that are not right in your house.

⁴⁴Verily, I say unto my servant Sidney Rigdon

that in some things he hath not kept the commandments
    concerning his children;
    therefore, first set in order thy house.

⁴⁵Verily, I say unto my servant Joseph Smith Jun.

(or, in other words, I will call you friends,
    for you are my friends,
    and ye shall have an inheritance with me;
⁴⁶I called you servants for the world's sake,
    and ye are their servants for my sake)—

⁴⁷and now, verily, I say unto Joseph Smith Jun.:

You have not kept the commandments
    and must needs stand rebuked before the Lord.
⁴⁸Your family must needs repent and forsake some things
    and give more earnest heed unto your sayings
    or be removed out of their place.

⁴⁹(What I say unto one I say unto all:

Pray always, lest that wicked one have power in you
    and remove you out of your place.)

⁵⁰My servant Newel K. Whitney, also,
    a bishop of my church,
hath need to be chastened
    and set in order his family
and see that they are more diligent and concerned at home
    and pray always,
    or they shall be removed out of their place.

⁵¹Now, I say unto you, my friends:

Let my servant Sidney Rigdon go on his journey and make haste,
    and also proclaim the acceptable year of the Lord
    and the gospel of salvation
    as I shall give him utterance;
and, by your prayer of faith, with one consent,
    I will uphold him.

⁵²And let my servants Joseph Smith Jun. and Frederick G. Williams
   make haste also,
   and it shall be given them,
   even according to the prayer of faith;
and inasmuch as you keep my sayings
   you shall not be confounded in this world,
   nor in the world to come.

⁵³And, verily, I say unto you

that it is my will
   that you should hasten to translate my scriptures
   and to obtain a knowledge of history
   and of countries
   and of kingdoms,
   of laws of God and man,

and all this for the salvation of Zion.

Amen.

COMMENTARY

Although most of the revelations recorded in the Doctrine and Covenants respond to particular questions, it is not known what question section 93 was intended to answer, but it is in effect a commentary on John 1:1–14. The Lord, who quotes John, is the main speaker in this piece, though he is introduced in the first line by a speaker that I have designated "Narrator." I have indicated by headings what I judge to be the identity of the speaker of each speech—the Narrator, the Lord, or John (the Apostle John or John the Baptist; commentators differ on that point, but it is irrelevant to the present purpose) as quoted by the Lord. The identity of the speaker of verses 29–38 is ambiguous. John clearly is the speaker of verse 28, but when does John stop and the Lord begin again? The Lord clearly is speaking in verse 39, and my reading is that the "but I" that begins that verse connects it with the preceding verses 29–38, those verses being the Lord's expansion on the words of John given in verse 28.

The central theme of the Lord's statement as a whole (including his quotations of John) is unity with God, with three subthemes: the unity of the Father and the Son (addressed in part i); the primal unity of man with God and the possibility of following a course similar to the

Son's, with the redeeming help of the Son, to achieve a new and more complex unity with God (addressed in part ii); and more immediate concerns with certain individuals and the failings that hinder them from achieving the proffered unity with God (addressed in part iii).

Part i begins (verses 1–2) with a promise that the faithful shall "see my face and know that I am," the fulfillment of which is not necessarily reserved for the next world. Section 93 is thus thematically in company with sections 76, 88, and 84 (which is not treated here), which emphasize the essential importance of the Holy Priesthood and its ordinances to the fulfillment of that promise, making section 93, along with those sections, a temple text. The final line of part i is a key to the paraphraseable intent of the whole text, as identifying the means by which men may obtain the promised blessing: following and being filled with the light that figuratively is Christ. From that identification of Christ with the divine light the text moves abruptly in verse 3 to the unity of Christ with the Father. That abruptness is not an incoherence, for, as has been noted, the unity that is the central theme of this section is achieved by the instrumentality of that light.

Verses 3–5 have a theological significance that is made more explicit by filling in the ellipses that follow "And the Father and I are one" as follows in an implied syntactic parallelism:

> And that I am in the Father,
>   and the Father in me,
> And the Father and I are one—
> [the Father and I are] the Father because
>   he gave me of his fulness
> and [the Father and I are] the Son because I was in the world
>   and made flesh my tabernacle
>   and dwelt among the sons of men.
> I was in the world and received of my Father,
>   and the works of him were plainly manifest;

Thus, the Son fully possesses the consciousness of the Father, and the Father fully possesses the consciousness of the Son. The words of Abinadi in Mosiah 15:1–4 are thus rescued from Nicene trinitarianism, for this is a unity in multiplicity—the individuality of Christ and the Father are preserved, but each is enlarged in the other; it is a case not of either-or (either one or separate) but of both-and:

God himself shall come down among the children of men, and shall redeem his people.

And because he dwelleth in flesh he shall be called the Son of God, and having subjected the flesh to the will of the Father, being the Father and the Son—

The Father, because he was conceived by the power of God; and the Son, because of the flesh; thus becoming the Father and the Son—

And they are one God, yea, the very Eternal Father of heaven and of earth.

The Savior then invokes the words of John (verses 6–17) to the effect that the Son was with the Father "before the world was," and he describes the process by which the Son in this world was restored to unity with the Father: "from grace to grace, / until he received a fulness." He then returns (verses 18–20) to the theme of the opening verses, explaining that, by a process similar to that through which the Savior went, men may obtain the same fulness.

The Savior begins part ii (in verses 21–22) by linking back to themes of part i: his presence with the Father at the beginning, and the possibility of man's partaking of the Father's glory; and then adding a definition of "the church of the Firstborn" as those who partake of that glory. There is an ambiguity in "church of the Firstborn." Christ is the Firstborn, and it is his church, that society of those who have obtained the promise of exaltation; but it is also the church comprised of the latter, who come to be treated by the Father as if they were the Son, becoming coinheritors with him of all things, being in him as he is in in the Father (see John 17:21). They also are, by adoption, the Firstborn, having taken upon them the name of Christ. Again, there is a case of both-and, of unity in multiplicity. Then the Savior goes on to reveal (in verses 23–39) another parallel between men and himself: not only can they come to enjoy the glory that he enjoys, but they were with the Father in the beginning as he was. What is meant by that is profoundly important and is one reason why section 93 is given primacy of place in this essay—it is a key text for arriving at the larger metaphysical frame in which a Latter-day Saint philosophy of art and a practical criticism and explication must ultimately find their place.

Joseph searched out not only the plan of salvation but also the essential nature of all reality; indeed, the two, in his thinking, could not be separated. He sought, in words of Elder John A. Widtsoe, "from out the universal mystery . . . the general, controlling laws, that proclaim order in the apparent chaos" (*A Rational Theology*, p. 1). He undertook what Sterling McMurrin describes as the task of metaphysics:

> Metaphysics is an attempt to answer the most basic questions which can be asked concerning the nature of reality. It has to do not with what in particular it is that in fact exists, but rather with the nature of existence as such, or with the general properties of whatever exists. It is concerned especially with ontological problems on the nature of being and cosmological problems on the structure of reality (*The Theological Foundations of the Mormon Religion/The Philosophical Foundations of the Mormon Religion*, p. 1).

Some of Joseph's key metaphysical insights are contained in verses 23–36 of section 93. If there is a single key metaphysical passage in section 93, it might well be this one (verses 29–31, directly quoting the official edition):

> Man was also in the beginning with God. Intelligence, or the light of truth, was not created or made, neither indeed can be.
> All truth is independent in that sphere in which God has placed it, to act for itself, as all intelligence also; otherwise there is no existence.
> Behold, here is the agency of man, and here is the condemnation of man; because that which was from the beginning is plainly manifest unto them, and they receive not the light.

Closely related to that passage are these, in the same section:

> Ye were also in the beginning with the Father; that which is Spirit, even the Spirit of truth;
> And truth is knowledge of things as they are, and as they were, and as they are to come;
> And whatsoever is more or less than this is the spirit of that wicked one who was a liar from the beginning.
> The Spirit of truth is of God. I am the Spirit of truth. . . . (Verses 23–26)

> For man is spirit. The elements are eternal, and spirit and element, inseparably connected, receive a fulness of joy;
> And when separated, man cannot receive a fulness of joy.

> The elements are the tabernacle of God; yea, man is the tabernacle of God, even temples; and whatsoever temple is defiled, God shall destroy that temple.
>
> The glory of God is intelligence, or, in other words, light and truth. (Verses 33–36).

The labor of Latter-day Saint writers to formulate a coherent metaphysic has largely consisted of attempts to interpret those passages. Section 93 (like all the rest of scripture) does not, in fact, present a systematic philosophy or cosmology. Rather, it presents loosely connected aphorisms, stated dogmatically, without reasoned defense or explanation, leaving the reader to discern relationships. This ambiguity is not a fault in the text, or in the thinking of Joseph Smith; rather, it reflects the nature of the problem of getting at ultimate realities by means of language. Indeed, it may not be possible to get closer, or much closer, to that toward which section 93 points aphoristically and suggestively, for language has its limits—analytical discourse would not have gotten any further. It also reflects the fact that Joseph was not a systematic philosopher or theologian but rather something more valuable—a prophet and a poet. Joseph certainly was aware of the limitations of the language he was using. He complained in a letter to William W. Phelps, dated November 27, 1832, of being limited by a "crooked broken scattered and imperfect language" (*Personal Writings of Joseph Smith,* p. 287). He might have sympathized with the sentiment expressed in lines of T. S. Eliot, in "Burnt Norton": "Words strain, / Crack and sometimes break, under the burden, / Under the tension, slip, slide, perish, / Decay with imprecision, will not stay in place, / Will not stay still." Thinking the problem further through, he might have recognized that no language could be adequate to the task, as any attempt to go to the end (or the beginning) of things linguistically is, in the words of Zen masters, like unto the attempt of a hand to grasp itself, an eye to see itself. The first link of any chain of reasoning or attempt at coherent exposition must necessarily be anchored in something that cannot be verbalized in any merely discursive way, and attempts so to verbalize it must necessarily end in paradox (as per Russell's Paradox and Göedel's incompleteness theorems). The use of this aphoristic, suggestive language with the approval of the Lord may be a caution against expecting too much from analytic, discursive, propositional language, and perhaps even a caution against becoming unduly entangled in metaphysical speculation.

I think that Joseph's meaning is made clearer by the repunctuation of D&C 93:23–26 as I have proposed:

Ye were also—
 in the beginning,
  with the Father—
that which is Spirit,
 even the Spirit of truth;

In other words, In the beginning, *you* were that which is Spirit, even the Spirit of truth—*as was the Father*.

I will step far enough into the philosophical tanglewood to submit that what Joseph arrived at in those verses, not by analytical reason but by intuition and divine illumination, is a kind of nondualism that would have been recognized by the philosophical Idealists of his time and by the Vedantic writers who influenced them. I am suggesting that Dr. Candadai Seshachari, a Hindu and a professor of English and Director of General Education at Weber State College, has correctly pointed the direction in which we should seek a path toward the metaphysic of section 93: "Mormons will be misunderstood and misrepresented as long as critics try to force traditional Christian meanings into the Mormon tenets and doctrines. It is far easier to approach the Mormon gospel through Hinduism than through Roman Catholicism, through the works of Sankara than those of St. Thomas Aquinas" (*Revelation: The Cohesive Element in International Mormonism*, p. 45). What I think Dr. Seshachari is getting at—and I think he is right—becomes clearer if a bit of Joseph's language in section 93 is translated into the language of the world's philosophers, if we read verse 30 as follows: "All *object* is independent in that sphere in which God has placed it, to act for itself, as all *subject* also; otherwise there is no existence"; or, perhaps, at a somewhat lower level of abstraction, "All *known* is independent in that sphere in which God has placed it, to act for itself, as all *knower* also; otherwise there is no existence." Joseph intuited a self-existing ground of existence, an Absolute, as some philosophers have called it, that he called "that which is Spirit, even the Spirit of truth," of which all the intelligences, including God himself, are expressions or manifestations. He did not ask the meaningless question "Why is there something and not nothing at all?" He accepted existence itself as a given, as it must be accepted (and he found in his intuition neither the *angst* of his contemporary Søren Kierkegaard nor the *nausée* of the later Jean-Paul Sartre; indeed, as he dictated the words in another place [italics added], "Men *are* that they might have joy" [2 Nephi 2:23]). He intuited that if there is no consciousness and nothing of which to *be* conscious there is no existence, and that consciousness and that-of-which-to-be-conscious—knower and known, subject and object—necessarily exist together as something like poles within the Absolute; that there is no consciousness—and therefore no existence—except of opposition, of *that* and *not that*; that there can be no consciousness without the opposition of permanence and change; that *being* is therefore an eternal process of *becoming*; that the Absolute is absolutely free to *become* in whatever forms of opposition it chooses (because what else is there to limit it or determine it?); that the personal God is the personification of the Absolute in relation to the inferior intelligences; that the inferior intelligences come into self-conscious being in something like an act of self-alienation by the Absolute as they are born as spirit children of the personal God; that the children of God possess agency because even in their alienated state they are of the same free stuff of the Absolute—and here is the agency of man; that the Absolute, in the person of God in relation to his children, seeks reintegration of its alienated self at a higher level of complexity, of fulness of being—of *joy*; that God's fundamental attitude toward his alienated parts is therefore love; and God's work and glory, therefore, is to bring to pass the immortality and eternal life of man (Abraham 1:39).

Yes, I am aware of the huge leaps of logic in the foregoing; that is why I submit that Joseph intuited all that, or something like that, rather than reasoned his way to it—for he was a prophet and a poet, not a German metaphysician. And I am aware that I have used much language that Joseph did not use—that is my clumsy attempt to say outright what Joseph was wise enough only to hint.

I have suggested that Joseph and the Idealist philosophers of the nineteenth century would have understood each other had they talked. I present here a few quotations from three of those philosophers to support that proposition. There is this from the *Biographia Literaria* of Samuel Taylor Coleridge, an approximate contemporary of Joseph Smith, in chapter 10: "God, not only as the ground of the universe by his essence, but as its maker and judge by his wisdom and holy will."

There is further parallel between Coleridge's thought and Joseph's through such statements as this, from chapter 8: "Body and spirit are therefore no longer absolutely heterogeneous, but may without any absurdity be supposed to be different modes, or degrees in perfection, of a common substratum." Compare D&C 131:7: "There is no such thing as immaterial matter. All spirit is matter, but it is more fine or pure." "Matter" in that verse might be taken as equivalent to Coleridge's substratum of body and spirit.

From Coleridge, chapter 9: "Truth is the correlative of Being. This again is no way conceivable, but by assuming as a postulate, that both are *ab initio* [from the beginning], identical and coinherent; that intelligence and being are reciprocally each other's substrate"; and from chapter 12: "An object is inconceivable without a subject as its antithesis." Compare D&C 93:30: "All truth is independent in that sphere in which God has placed it, to act for itself, as all intelligence also; otherwise there is no existence"; and D&C 93:33: "The elements are eternal."

From chapter 12: "Intelligence or self-consciousness is impossible, except by and in a will. The self-conscious spirit therefore is a will; and freedom must be assumed as a ground of philosophy, and can never be deduced from it." Compare D&C 93:30–31: "All truth is independent in that sphere in which God has placed it, to act for itself, as all intelligence also; otherwise there is no existence. Behold, here is the agency of man."

From chapter 12: "We begin with the I KNOW MYSELF, in order to end with the absolute I AM. We proceed from the SELF, in order to lose and find all self in GOD" (1:186). Compare D&C 93:23 (as I have emended the punctuation): "Ye also were—in the beginning, with God—that which is Spirit, even the Spirit of truth."

Arthur Schopenhauer, another contemporary of Joseph, wrote in *The World as Will and Representation:*

> No truth is more certain, more independent of all others, and less in need of proof than this, namely that everything that exists for knowledge, and hence the whole of this world, is only object in relation to the subject, perception of the perceiver, in a word, representation. . . . Therefore the world as representation . . . has two essential, necessary, and inseparable halves. The one half is the *object*. . . . the other half, the subject. . . . Therefore these halves are inseparable even in thought, for each of the two has meaning and existence only through and for the other; each exists with the other and vanishes with it (p. 3).

Again, compare that to D&C 93: 30–31: "All truth is independent in that sphere in which God has placed it, to act for itself, as all intelligence also; otherwise there is no existence. Behold, here is the agency of man."

Schopenhauer found parallel with his own thinking in that of "the sages of India": "The fundamental tenet of the Vedânta school consisted not in denying the existence of matter, that is, of solidity, impenetrability, and extended figure (to deny which would be lunacy), but in correcting the popular notion of it, and in contending that it has no essence independent of mental perception; that existence and perceptibility are convertible terms" (3–4).

Then there is this:

> From all these considerations the reader has now gained in the abstract, and hence in clear and certain terms, a knowledge which everyone possesses directly in the concrete, namely as feeling. This is the knowledge that the inner nature of his own phenomenon, which manifests itself to him as representation both through his actions and through the permanent substratum of these in his body, is his *will*. . . . He will recognize that same will not only in those phenomena that are quite similar to his own, in men and animals, as their innermost nature, but continued reflection will lead him to recognize the force that shoots and vegetates in the plant, indeed the force by which the crystal is formed, the force that turns the magnet to the North Pole, the force whose shock he encounters from the contact of metals of different kinds, the force that appears in the elective affinities of matter as repulsion and attraction, separation and union, and finally even gravitation, which acts so powerfully in all matter, pulling the stone to earth and the earth to the sun; all these he will recognize as different only in the phenomenon, but the same according to their inner nature. He will recognize them all as that which is immediately known to him so intimately and better than everything else, and where it appears most distinctly is called *will* (pp. 109–10).

Once more, "here is the agency of man" (and of everything else; but that is beyond the scope of this essay).

The thinking of the likes of the Vedantists, Schopenhauer, and Coleridge entered into the stream of American thought by way of the Transcendentalists, outstandingly Ralph Waldo Emerson, from whose essay "The Over-Soul" I extract but a few lines to make the point: ". . . that Unity, that Over-soul, within which every man's particular being is contained and made one with all other. . . . We live in succession, in division, in parts, in wise silence; the universal beauty, to which every part and particle is equally related; the eternal ONE. . . . We see the world piece by piece, as the sun, the moon, the animal, the tree; but the whole, of which these are the shining parts, is the soul" (pp. 155–56).

There is, of course, no evidence of influence or borrowing between Vedantists, Schopenhauer, Coleridge, or Emerson, on the one hand, and Joseph Smith on the other. He arrived at his insights independently of them, and they of him. One of my purposes here for presenting the excerpts from the philosophers quoted above, with whom Joseph in section 93 seems to have an affinity, is to illuminate some implications and ramifications of section 93—if *intelligence* and *truth* and *that which is Spirit* are correctly "translated" as I have proposed.

But there is more to section 93 than theme; there is the "how" it says "what" it says about its theme. For one thing, section 93 (like all of these texts) "means" indirectly through its use of biblical language. As noted by Roger K. Petersen, in "Joseph Smith Prophet-Poet," vocabulary and phraseology in the Doctrine and Covenants, including section 93, frequently echo the King James Bible. This is not mere imitation or plagiarism, however; rather, it maintains continuity with the prophetic and literary traditions of the Bible and also implies meaning. In most cases, words and phrases that parallel those of the Bible are recombined or given new meaning by being given a new context. That new context frequently includes new language, for Joseph introduces much nonbiblical language, thereby expanding and enriching the language, and thereby the content, of sacred discourse. The new and the old are joined seamlessly, so smoothly that only a very exceptional reader could discern one from the other without constant recourse to a concordance. The old is woven like threads into the fabric of the new, which, in Latter-day Saint belief, is a restoration of the oldest of all to wholeness. To say this in another way: Joseph Smith does not plagiarize biblical language, any more than any speaker of English plagiarizes when he speaks new sentences with familiar words and phrases from, say, Shakespeare; rather, "King James" is to Joseph a language, of which he has an exhaustive knowledge and which he speaks fluently and creatively. He does not use only the more common biblical language, what might be "picked up" by casual hearing, but also seizes upon phrases that are rare in the Bible, thereby calling attention to them and investing them with larger meaning. These poems (and all of the Doctrine and Covenants) should be read with constant reference to a concordance.

Some remarks in a discussion of biblical poetry by Robert Alter on "originality" or its lack in the Bible itself are relevant here. He writes that "stock imagery . . . is the staple of biblical poetry" (*The Art of Biblical Poetry*, p. 190). He further observes that there is an advantage in working with such conventional figures, that "our attention tends to be guided through the metaphoric vehicle to the tenor for which the vehicle was introduced." The creative accomplishment of the biblical poet is often in the "intensive development" of the stock imagery. Discussing the Psalms, Alter writes:

> Our own post-Romantic disposition to originality in literature may lead to a certain perplexity about how to think of a collection where in any given genre a dozen or more poems seem to be saying the same thing, often with more or less the same metaphors and sometimes even with some of the same phrasing. What I think we need to be more attuned to as readers is the nuanced individual character—'originality' in fact may not be the relevant concept—of different poems reflecting the same genre and even many of the same formulaic devices. There are abundant instances in later poetic tradition, as in Arabic and Hebrew Poetry of medieval Spain, Petrarchan love poetry, much English Augustan verse, where the power of the individual poem is meant to be felt precisely in such a fine recasting of the conventional, and that is what we ought to be able to discern more minutely in the psalms (pp. 112–13).

Within the biblical tradition, the only literary tradition with which Joseph was very familiar, the question to be asked is, what has Joseph done with the conventions (and not only those of language, as shall be seen)? The answer is that he has done quite a lot. He has surpassed the biblical poets in the boldness with which he reworks old traditions and conventions. He does with the tradition what Ezra Pound said the poet should do: "Make it new!"

I present a few examples here from section 93. Consider the first words:

Verily, thus saith the Lord:

It shall come to pass

"Verily" is immediately recognizable as a biblical word, and "thus saith the Lord" and "it shall come to pass" are very common biblical phrases, in both old and new testaments. The effect here is not only to claim divine authority for what follows but also to place the text within the prophetic and literary tradition of the Bible. The next few lines then draw together widely scattered biblical phrases into a coherent statement of a program for achieving the divine vision.

> that every soul

"Every soul" occurs several times in the Bible, with the meaning of "every person." The word "soul" is tinged with other meanings for Latter-day Saints, as it is used in the Book of Mormon to mean the seat of the deepest feelings and desires (as in 2 Nephi 4:15–16), or as something like "spirit" or "conscious faculty" (as in Alma 36:15), or particularly as what is called "spirit" in other scriptures of the Restoration (as in in Alma 40:43); and in D&C 88:15 it is defined as the combined "spirit and the body."

> who forsaketh his sins

"Forsaketh" occurs several times in the Bible, but only once in context with "sins," and then not directly: "He that covereth his sins shall not prosper: but whoso confesseth and forsaketh them shall have mercy" (Proverbs 28:13).

> and cometh unto me,

This phrase occurs only once biblically, in John 6:45: "Every man therefore that hath heard, and hath learned of the Father, cometh unto me." More common is the similar usage exemplified in Matthew 11:28, "Come unto me, all ye that labour and are heavy laden, and I will give you rest," which typically is read as referring to the challenges and vicissitudes of life, but can be read as referring to the futile labor of sinful man to rid himself of the burden of sin without the help of Christ. Pairing "come unto me" with "forsaketh his sins" thus emphasizes the fact that the process of sanctification—of being cleansed of sinfulness—is not a process of self-reformation but requires an active turning to Christ that is inseparable from the forsaking of sin and enables the forsaking of sin.

> and calleth on my name,

That phrase is similar to a biblical one that occurs only once: "they [my people] shall call on my name, and I will hear them" (Zecharaiah 13:9), implying that calling on God's name by modern disciples will have a similarly positive outcome.

and obeyeth my voice,

The similar phrase "obey my voice" occurs several times in the Bible, as in Exodus 12:5: "Now therefore, if ye will obey my voice indeed, and keep my covenant, then ye shall be a peculiar treasure unto me above all people: for all the earth is mine."

and keepeth my commandments,

"Keep my commandments" is common in the Old Testament, but occurs only twice in the new—"If ye love me, keep my commandments" (John 14:15) and "If ye keep my commandments, ye shall abide in my love; even as I have kept my Father's commandments, and abide in his love" (John 15:10)—notably in connection with the sermon and prayer in which the hope is offered that men may become one in Christ as Christ is one in the Father.

Shall see my face

This occurs relevantly in Exodus 33:20: "And he said, thou canst not see my face: for there shall no man see me, and live"; and also John 1:18: "No man hath seen God at any time; the only begotten Son, which is in the bosom of the Father, he hath declared him." The present text neatly qualifies both of those verses, specifying the conditions under which a person in fact can see the face of God and live.

and know that I am;

That phrase recalls Exodus 12:14, "And God said unto Moses, I AM THAT I AM," implying that the faithful can know personally the "I AM" spoken of there.

The next verses, 2–18, recall John 1:1–19. John 1:19 indicates that the foregoing verses in John 1 represent the record of John, and section 93 confirms that and apparently restores in verses 2–18 (a passage too long to be repeated here; the reader is referred to the poem) a presumably more pure version of John's record. Then there is this in verse 19:

> I give unto you these sayings
>   that you may understand and know how to worship,
>   and know what you worship,
> That you may come unto the Father in my name,
>   and in due time receive of his fulness.

That verse recalls John 4:22–23, in the story of Jesus' encounter with the Samaritan woman at the well: "Ye worship ye know not what: we know what we worship. . . . But the hour cometh, and now is, when the true worshippers shall worship the Father in spirit and in truth." The implication is that a more correct knowledge of God is being restored in the current dispensation, as Jesus was restoring it to the Samaritan woman and her contemporaries. That is further a hint that the sectarian world of Joseph's time is in a state of apostasy and corruption of doctrine analogous to that of the Samaritans with their own mixture of scripture with the philosophies of men.

Our understanding of the nature of what we worship is enhanced by the revealed understanding of man's primeval identity with what we worship. The end of verse 19, of course, parallels John 1:16, "And of his fulness have all we received, and grace for grace," setting up what comes next:

> For if you keep my commandments
>   you shall receive of his fulness,
>   and be glorified in me as I am in the Father;
> Therefore, I say unto you,
>   you shall receive grace for grace.

The next major part of section 93 expands on the idea of being "with God" (John 1:1), and on what Jesus was "getting at" in the intercessory prayer:

> And now, O Father, glorify thou me with thine own self with the glory which I had with thee before the world was. . . .
> I pray for them . . . which thou has given me; for they are thine;
> And all mine are thine, and thine are mine; and I am glorified in them. . . .
> That they all may be one; as thou, Father, art in me, and I in thee, that they also may be one in us. . . .

> And the glory which thou gavest me I have given them: that they
>   may be one, even as we are one:
> I in them, and thou in me, that they may be made perfect in one
>   . . . (John 17:9–22).

The Savior is offering to his faithful disciples the possibility of attaining to the same unity with the Father that he himself enjoys—the fulness.

Most of the following, already discussed above, is new language:

> The Spirit of truth is of God;
>   I am the Spirit of truth;
>
> and John bore record of me, saying:

JOHN:

> He received a fulness of truth,
>   yea, even of all truth;
> and no man receiveth a fulness
>   unless he keepeth his commandments.
> He that keepeth his commandments receiveth truth and light
>   until he is glorified in truth and knoweth all things.

THE LORD:

> Man was also—
>   in the beginning—
>   with God;
> intelligence,
>   or the light of truth,
> was not created or made,
>   neither indeed can be.
> All truth is independent in that sphere in which God has placed it,
>   to act for itself,
> as all intelligence also;
>   otherwise there is no existence.
> Behold, here is the agency of man,
>   and here is the condemnation of man,
> because that which was from the beginning
>   is plainly manifest unto them,
>   and they receive not the light,

and every man whose spirit receiveth not the light
  is under condemnation;

"Receive" and "receiveth" are key words in that passage, and they occur relevantly in the following biblical passages:

"But the natural man receiveth not the things of the spirit of god: for they are foolishness unto him: neither can he know them, because they are spiritually discerned" (1 Corinthians 2:14).

"Verily, verily, I say unto thee, we speak that we do know, and testify that we have seen; and ye receive not our witness" (John 3:11).

Continuing with section 93:

For man is spirit,
  the elements are eternal,
And spirit and element,
  inseparably connected,
  receive a fulness of joy;
And when separated,
  man cannot receive a fulness of joy.

Most of the language is new, but meaning is lent to those lines by Psalm 16:11, "In thy presence is fulness of joy," for this text is about preparing to dwell in the presence of God, in new unity with God.

The elements are the tabernacle of God;
  yea, man is the tabernacle of God,
  even temples;

"Tabernacle of God" occurs once in the Bible, in Revelation 21:3, "And I heard a great voice out of heaven saying, behold, the tabernacle of God is with men, and he will dwell with them, and they shall be his people, and God himself shall be with them, and be their God." The meaning there is that Christ is the "tabernacle of God," for the Father dwells in him. Section 93:35 goes further to make all "the elements," and particularly men themselves, the tabernacle of God, presumably by the presence in them of his consciousness, and ultimately their nondualistic identity with his consciousness. An implication is that all the material universe, and especially the human body, should be treated as possessing the sacredness of a temple.

> And whatsoever temple is defiled,
> God shall destroy that temple.

Those words recall 1 Corinthians 3:17, "If any man defile the temple of God, him shall God destroy; for the temple of God is holy, which temple ye are."

> The glory of God is intelligence,
>   or, in other words, light and truth;
>   light and truth forsake that evil one.
> Every spirit of man was innocent in the beginning;
>   and God having redeemed man from the fall,
>   men became again, in their infant state, innocent before God
> And that wicked one cometh and taketh away light and truth,

Biblical words—"glory," "light," "truth," "forsake," "evil one," "spirit," "in the beginning," "redeemed," "fall," "wicked one"—saturate that passage, but the final product is new, and practically the same can be said of all of part iii.

The foregoing is more than enough to make it evident that section 93, and the same applies to all the Doctrine and Covenants, needs to be read with a Bible concordance in hand, because Joseph's use of biblical language always means something, and because it is important to know when he is departing from biblical language. There is more, however—the "form" into which this language is cast. When section 93 (again, like all the other texts) is read aloud as I have suggested, with a pause, longer or shorter, at the end of each verset, it demonstrates a rhythmic quality, a cadence, a pattern in the stress on words and the rise and fall of pitch and volume in the voice. This cadence is sufficient justification for calling it "poetic," for, as Barbara Hernstein Smith observes, "As soon as we perceive that a verbal sequence has a sustained rhythm, that it is formally structured according to a continuously operating principle of organization, we know that we are in the presence of poetry. . . . and we respond to it accordingly . . ., expecting certain effects from it and not others, granting certain conventions to it and not others" (*Poetic Closure*, p. 23). Smith further observes: "One of the most significant effects of meter . . . in poetry is simply to inform the reader that he is being confronted by poetry and not by anything else. ... Meter serves, in other words, as a frame for the poem, separating it from a 'ground' of less highly structured speech or sound." The language of section 93 is not metered, but it is cadenced, following natural patterns of speech and breath, probably in part a consequence of the way in which it was composed and delivered, dictated thought unit by thought unit. That cadence performs the same function as the stricter rhythm of meter, to "frame" the text, to unify it and give it a life of its own, as something separate from its surroundings. A comparison of the style of these poems with the language that surrounds them in the primary sources will confirm that the poems are indeed set apart from their surroundings.

Cadence combines with vocabulary and phraseology to give section 93 a biblical "feel," but it is employed creatively in a manner that approaches skillfully employed modern free verse. One of its uses is to express meaning by variation from the regular or expected pattern. For example, the versets of the first three verses are terse, tight, to the point. Then, when the subject turns to "fulness," they become more relaxed, longer—more "full."

In that relaxation is a sense that the Son has come to rest in the Father, and the Father in the Son. That pattern of terseness, tightness, followed by fulness and relaxation, is repeated in 7–14 and 15–17, which also end with the notion of fulness. Verses 18–20 also treat of "fulness," but in this case the "fulness" of syntax comes in the middle, making it possible to use the "punchier" shorter lines to emphasize "grace" (and it surely is no accident that the word *grace* gets prominence of place as the final word of that section).

This same contrast is used in the overall structure of the text: after the relatively intense doctrinal instruction of the first two parts, the speaker seems to relax a bit and assume a more conversational tone with those whom he calls his "friends." The versets of part iii are longer, looser. The conversational tone is further enhanced by the parenthetical digression in verses 45–46, after which the broken thread of thought is taken up again by the repetition at the beginning of verse 47 of the initial words of verse 45.

Modulation within versets and lines is illustrated by verses 2–3:

> And that I am the true light
>   that lighteth every man
>   that cometh into the world;

> And that I am in the Father,
> and the Father in me,

Stress falls naturally on "I" and "true light," tying them together; but somewhat less on "true light," leaving the greatest stress on the "I" that refers directly to Christ. In the next verset, the greatest stress falls on the first syllable of "lighteth," emphasizing the "light" that is a key to the unity with God promised in this text; then lesser but equal stress falls on the first syllable of "every" and "man," emphasizing that each and every individual born on the earth receives the invitation to unity with God. In the next line, "I" and "Father," and "Father" and "me," respectively, demand equal stress, emphasizing the oneness of Father and Son.

Verse 5 contains an odd construction, "and the works of him were plainly manifest." "His works" would be more idiomatic; but that would tend to place the emphasis on "works," and the construction that is given appropriately emphasizes "him," the Father.

Finally, this:

> And the Holy Ghost descended upon him in the form of a dove
> and sat upon him,

In the relaxed amplitude of the first verset, there is a feeling of floating as the dove descends, ended by the somewhat abrupt finality of the short second verset as the dove comes to a stop.

Closely related to the cadence of section 93 is syntactic, verbal, and semantic parallelism. As is well known, parallelism is the most characteristic prosodic device of biblical poetry, and section 93 (once more, like all of these texts) remains within that tradition, but again, as with vocabulary and cadence, it overflows the biblical conventions. By such couplets as "he hath put my brethren far from me, / and mine acquaintance are verily estranged from me" (Job 19:3), biblical verse particularizes, intensifies, defines, expands, and advances narrative, in small increments, as Alter describes its uses. Alter recognizes certain constraints of such parallelism: "The two basic operations of specification and heightening within the parallelistic line lead to an incipiently narrative structure of minute concatenations, on the one hand, and to a climactic structure of thematic intensifications, on the other" (pp. 62–63). He observes that "a poet who felt moved, let us say, to celebrate the teeming variety and vastness of the human and natural landscape would . . . need a kind of poetic vehicle that was more expansive, allowing for free-flowing catalogues and effects of asymmetry and improvisation—would need, in short, something like Whitmanesque free verse" (p. 62). Joseph, in fact, has moved on to such a vehicle, though not having become quite so free as Whitman. No couplet like the one just quoted occurs in section 93. Frequently, moreover, any kind of parallelism altogether breaks down as in this line, in which the versets group together only because they are clauses or phrases in the same sentence:

> And it shall come to pass that,
> > if you are faithful,
> > you shall receive the fulness of the record of John.

That fact causes true parallelisms to stand out, emphasizing the importance of passages, as they do occur, as in verses 1–4:

> NARRATOR:
> Verily, thus saith the Lord:
>
> THE LORD:
> It shall come to pass that every soul
> > who forsaketh his sins,
> > and cometh unto me,
> > and calleth on my name,
> > and obeyeth my voice,
> > and keepeth my commandments
> shall see my face
> > and know that I am and that I am the true light
> > > that lighteth every man
> > > that cometh into the world,
> > and that I am in the Father,
> > > and the Father in me,
> > > and the Father and I are one—
> > the Father because he gave me of his fulness
> > > and the Son because I was in the world
> > > and made flesh my tabernacle
> > > and dwelt among the sons of men.

Into one long sentence is packed a great deal of information about what is required for a mortal to come to know God, all as a complex, unified thought, with series of syntactically parallel phrases all hung on the initial "It shall come to pass that." Something similar occurs in verse 53, with the prepositional phrases hung on "to obtain a knowledge of history":

> and to obtain a knowledge of history,
> and of countries,
> and of kingdoms,
> of laws of God and man,

Elaborations of this sort through syntactical parallels in a kind of list are characteristic of the Doctrine and Covenants. In the case of section 93, these series of parallel short phrases are imbedded among passages of longer lines or shorter parallel series, or a combination of both, which has the effect of calling attention to them and concentrating the mind on a certain theme.

Interlinear parallelism is as important in section 93 as intralinear, unifying and ordering thought through longer passages. Note the series of parallel phrases introducing stanzas: "And John saw and bore record" (verse 6), "And I, John, bear record" (verse 11), "And I John saw" (verse 12), "And I, John, bear record" (verse 15), "And I, John, bear record" (verse 16). The same use of parallelism occurs in part iii.

Then there is the mirror-image parallelism known as *chiasm*. Chiasm is exemplified in a simple way by these phrases from Samuel Johnson (in "The Vanity of Human Wishes"): "by day the frolic, and the dance by night," which may be presented diagrammatically as follows:

> 2) by day
>   1) the frolic
>   1) and the dance
> 2) by night

Much work has already been done to identify chiasms in the Doctrine and Covenants—I am heavily indebted to H. Clay Gorton, Charles Francis King, Richard C. Shipp, and William H. Brugger for identifying and laying out the chiasmic patterns in detail. I do not wish to duplicate their work, to which the reader is referred, in these pages; a more general approach must serve here.

Ten chiasms occur in section 93. It is notable that no chiasms occur in part iii, where a generally more relaxed conversational attitude is suddenly assumed; the absence of that structuring contributes to the relaxation. All of the chiasms occur in the two sections where doctrine is concentrated, and most of them, six of the ten, occur in the section that presents new doctrine. They serve to concentrate the attention where the most important teaching is to occur. The ten chiasms with their central points (somewhat paraphrased) are as follows:

Chiasm 1, verses 4–5: Christ (in whom the Father dwelt) dwelt in the flesh among the sons of men.

Chiasm 2, verse 6: the fulness of John's record, testifying of "fulness" of Christ's glory, is yet to be revealed.

Chiasm 3, verses 12–14: Christ continued from grace to grace until he received of the fulness.

Chiasm 4, verse 15: the Holy Ghost descended upon Christ in the form of a dove.

Chiasm 5, verses 21–22: Those who are begotten of Christ become partakers of the glory of the Firstborn.

Chiasm 6, verses 23–26: untruth is of the devil.

Chiasm 7, verses 27–28: Obeying the commandments of God is necessary to obtaining a fulness of truth.

Chiasm 8, verses 29–30: Intelligence and the "truth" that it knows exist eternally (there is therefore no escape from the consequences of rejecting truth).

Chiasm 9, verses 31–32: Truth is offered to all men, but many reject it.

Chiasm 10, verse 35: A human "temple" that defiles itself by rejection of truth, by disobedience, will be in some sense "destroyed."

That is a coherent summary of the probationary nature of human mortality, and a thematic summary of section 93. It seems notable that this device for emphasizing main points is used most intensively in the section that presents the greatest doctrinal development, and that that section is in the center of the whole composition. I am unable to argue that there is any organic relationship between the paraphraseable idea of each chiasm and the form as such of the chiasm (though that does not mean that chiasm as such does not "mean" something presentationally; I return to that point in the concluding remarks), but when one "gets the hang" of reading it, a chiasm supplies a certain aesthetic pleasure in its symmetry, a sense of completion in going deeply into something and returning to come to rest.

It should also be noted that there is more to chiasm than rigid symmetry in the ascending and descending elements. Below are the corresponding ascending and descending elements of the chiasm in

93:4–5 matched together in what reveal themselves to be two-verset, parallel lines, exhibiting elaboration and intensification in the classic biblical style; the view on the way out is not exactly the view on the way in:

> the Father because he gave me of his fulness . . .
> and the works of him were plainly manifest.

> and the Son because I was in the world . . .
> I was in the world and received of my Father,

> and made flesh my tabernacle . . .
> and dwelt among the sons of men;

I leave it to the reader to conduct this same exercise with other chiasms in these works, particularly in section 76. It will be rewarded.

As so far read, section 93 is an example of rhetoric, with "content" reinforced by "form," albeit "poetic" form. There is more, however.

Gross elements of the structure of section 93, the three main parts of the text, have already been noted. Section i treats of the supreme unity toward which the mortal servant-friends of section iii are laboring; section iii treats of the creative complication of the Spirit/Absolute in inferior selves that seek reunion with the Spirit/Absolute; section ii relates to both i and iii by revealing the true identity of those servant-friends as manifestations, creative in themselves, of the Spirit/Absolute (and thus also the multiplicity in unity of the Spirit/Absolute—their both-and relationship), as children of God and also the path by which reunification, at a higher level of complexity and thereby at a greater density, richness, of being can be obtained by the yet imperfect mortals of section iii. A dynamic of countermotion (the term used by John Ciardi in *How Does a Poem Mean?*) that creates and resolves certain tensions within the text operates among the three parts, with one fulcrum (Ciardi's term) between ii and iii, and another between i and ii. Section i reaffirms and expands the doctrine taught in John 1–14, but not so far as to break with traditional Christian doctrine. Then, in section ii, it is as if the Lord says by implication, "You have already known essentially what I have just told you, but now let me give you a deeper understanding of things." That countermotion is signaled by a change in style, in the increased frequency of chiasm and in the concentration of short, aphoristic versets through which a new metaphysical understanding is indicated. At the fulcrum between ii and iii, the Lord suddenly shifts to calling certain individuals' attention to the fact that they are falling short of the requirements for entering into the divine unity, and there a tension, a counterthrust, is created, as failure to obtain the proffered blessing suddenly becomes a real possibility; but the tension is quickly relieved by the hope implied in the final words—to see God, as promised in the first lines upon certain conditions, is still a real possibility, and that is where the text ends, on hope. That passage is more relaxed, more conversational, with longer, looser lines and versets, after the intensity of section ii. Section iii almost trails off from the theme of unity, as particular instructions and admonitions are given to certain individuals, but it is brought abruptly back by the very last verset: "and all this for the salvation of Zion." Zion, in the "works of Joseph Smith," is a society in which the inhabitants are "of one heart and one mind" in Christ (Moses 7:18)—the last word of the text both gives it closure and ties it back to the theme of unity and thus closes a circle that begins with the first section. There is another fulcrum, the main one in this text, at that last word, *Zion*. It has come "out of nowhere," suddenly suggesting a great expansion on the theme; but, though it points back to the beginning of the work, it also points forward to something more that is not developed. It stands between what comes before and a pregnant silence.

Moreover, concentrated in the microcosm of section 93 is the whole drama of "the great plan of happiness"—primeval unity of man with God, an initial alienation with birth as God's "spirit children," a deeper and potentially more complete alienation by sin, hope offered through the atonement of Christ, the final outcome held in suspension awaiting the exercise of human agency.

And there is something more. This is a poetic drama. In the first line, "Verily, thus saith the Lord," the author steps back and a character known as "the Lord" steps out onto an imaginary stage and delivers a monologue. This monologue is revealing of character. At the beginning, the Lord presents himself as the equal of the Father, vastly superior to man. At the end he is conversing in a relaxed manner with his friends; he is the risen Lord who prepared a meal on shore of the Galilee and invited his friends to join him—but knowing that the response to that invitation will be an exercise of their own agency, that agency having been acknowledged within the poem itself as being bound up in the nature of very existence. At the beginning, he is the remote and all-powerful God of Genesis 1 who brings a world into being by his word alone; at the end he is the God of Genesis 2 who works with his hands in mud to create man and walks and talks with him in the Garden—who are, of course, the same God, under different aspects, and a not quite omnipotent God who himself hangs in hopeful suspense awaiting the exercise of human agency. It is the tension of these polarities, with their crossmotion between the poles, with final resolution deferred but hope offered in the last word, that underlies and fundamentally structures, and thus unifies, the whole work. In these crossmotions—which are presented as occurring within the mind of God himself, revealing a dramatic moment in the life of God himself—section 93 rises from mere rhetoric to the status of poem, to something described by Cleanth Brooks: "It is in terms of structure that we must describe poetry. . . . The structure meant is a structure of meanings, evaluations, and interpretations; and the principle of unity which informs it seems to be one of balancing and harmonizing connotations, attitudes, and meanings" (*The Well-Wrought Urn*, pp. 194–95).

Doctrine and Covenants 76

i

PROLOGUE

NARRATOR:

¹Hear, O ye heavens,
 and give ear, O earth,
 and rejoice ye inhabitants thereof;
for the Lord is God,
 and beside him there is no Savior.
²Great is his wisdom,
 marvelous are his ways,
 and the extent of his doings none can find out.
³His purposes fail not,
 neither are there any who can stay his hand.
⁴From eternity to eternity he is the same,
 and his years never fail.

⁵For thus saith the Lord:

THE LORD:

I, the Lord, am merciful and gracious unto those who fear me
 and delight to honor those who serve me
 in righteousness and in truth unto the end.
⁶Great shall be their reward,
 and eternal shall be their glory,
⁷and to them will I reveal all mysteries,
 yea, all the hidden mysteries of my kingdom from days of old;

and for ages to come will I make known unto them
   the good pleasure of my will
      concerning all things pertaining to my kingdom.
⁸Yea, even the wonders of eternity shall they know,
   and things to come will I show them,
      even the things of many generations,
⁹and their wisdom shall be great
   and their understanding reach to heaven,
and before them the wisdom of the wise shall perish,
   and the understanding of the prudent shall come to naught;
¹⁰for by my Spirit will I enlighten them,
   and by my power will I make known unto them
      the secrets of my will,
yea, even those things which eye has not seen,
   nor ear heard,
      nor yet entered into the heart of man.

ii

A VISION OF THE SON

NARRATOR:

¹¹We, Joseph Smith, Jun., and Sidney Rigdon,
   being in the Spirit on the sixteenth day of February,
   in the year of our Lord one thousand eight hundred and thirty-two,
¹²by the power of the Spirit our eyes were opened
   and our understandings were enlightened
so as to see and understand the things of God,
¹³   even those things which were from the beginning,
   before the world was,
which were ordained of the Father
   through his Only Begotten Son,
who was in the bosom of the Father,
   even from the beginning,
¹⁴   of whom we bear record;
and the record which we bear
   is the fulness of the gospel of Jesus Christ,
      who is the Son,
      whom we saw

Doctrine and Covenants 76

and with whom we conversed in the heavenly vision.
¹⁵For while we were doing the work of translation
   which the Lord had appointed unto us,
we came to the twenty-ninth verse of the fifth chapter of John,
   which was given unto us as follows,
¹⁶speaking of the resurrection of the dead,
   concerning those who shall hear the voice of the Son of Man:

THE GOSPEL ACCORDING TO JOHN:

¹⁷And shall come forth;
   they who have done good, in the resurrection of the just,
   and they who have done evil, in the resurrection of the unjust.

NARRATOR:

¹⁸Now, this caused us to marvel,
   for it was given unto us of the Spirit;
¹⁹and, while we meditated upon these things,
   the Lord touched the eyes of our understandings,
and they were opened,
   and the glory of the Lord shone round about,
²⁰and we beheld the glory of the Son,
   on the right hand of the Father,
and received of his fulness,
²¹   and saw the holy angels
   and them who are sanctified before his throne,
worshiping God and the Lamb,
   who worship him forever and ever;
²²and now, after the many testimonies which have been given of him,
   this is the testimony, last of all, which we give of him:
   that he lives!
²³For we saw him,
   even on the right hand of God;
and we heard the voice bearing record
   that he is the Only Begotten of the Father,
²⁴that by him,
   and through him,
   and of him
the worlds are and were created,
   and the inhabitants thereof
   are begotten sons and daughters unto God.

A VISION OF LUCIFER

NARRATOR:

²⁵ And this we saw also,
  and bear record,
that an angel of God
  who was in authority in the presence of God,
  who rebelled against the Only Begotten Son,
  whom the Father loved,
  and who was in the bosom of the Father,
was thrust down from the presence of God and the Son,
²⁶ and was called Perdition,
for the heavens wept over him—
  he was Lucifer, a son of the morning,
²⁷ and we beheld, and lo,
  he is fallen!
  is fallen!
  even a son of the morning!
²⁸ And while we were yet in the Spirit,
  the Lord commanded us that we should write the vision;
for we beheld Satan,
  that old serpent,
  even the devil,
who rebelled against God
  and sought to take the kingdom of our God and his Christ;
²⁹ wherefore, he maketh war with the saints of God
  and encompasseth them round about.

A VISION OF THE KINGDOM OF LUCIFER

NARRATOR:

³⁰ And we saw a vision of the suffering of those
  with whom he made war and overcame,
  for thus came the voice of the Lord unto us:

THE LORD:

³¹ Thus saith the Lord concerning all those who know my power,
  and have been made partakers thereof,

and suffered themselves through the power of the devil
> to be overcome
> and to deny the truth and defy my power:

³²they are they who are the sons of perdition,
> of whom I say that it had been better for them
> never to have been born;

³³for they are vessels of wrath,
> doomed to suffer the wrath of God
> with the devil and his angels in eternity;

³⁴concerning whom I have said there is no forgiveness,
> in this world
> nor in the world to come,

³⁵having denied the Holy Spirit after having received it,
> and having denied the Only Begotten Son of the Father,

having crucified him unto themselves
> and put him to an open shame.

³⁶These are they who shall go away into the lake of fire and brimstone
> with the devil and his angels,

³⁷and the only ones on whom the second death shall have any power;

³⁸ yea, verily, the only ones who shall not be redeemed
> in the due time of the Lord,
> after the sufferings of his wrath;

³⁹for all the rest shall be brought forth by the resurrection of the dead,
> through the triumph and the glory of the Lamb,
> who was slain,
> who was in the bosom of the Father before the worlds were made.

NARRATOR:

⁴⁰And this is the gospel,
> the glad tidings,
> which the voice out of the heavens bore record unto us, that:

THE LORD:

⁴¹He came into the world,
> even Jesus,

to be crucified for the world,
> and to bear the sins of the world,

and to sanctify the world,
> and to cleanse it from all unrighteousness;

⁴²that through him all might be saved
   whom the Father had put into his power
   and made by him;
⁴³who glorifies the Father
   and saves all the works of his hands,
except those sons of perdition,
   who deny the Son after the Father has revealed him.
⁴⁴Wherefore, he saves all except them;
   they shall go away into everlasting punishment,
which is endless punishment,
   which is eternal punishment,
to reign with the devil and his angels in eternity,
   where their worm dieth not,
   and the fire is not quenched,
   which is their torment;
⁴⁵and the end thereof,
   neither the place thereof,
   nor their torment,
   no man knows;
⁴⁶neither was it revealed,
   neither is,
   neither will be revealed unto man,
   except to them who are made partakers thereof.
⁴⁷Nevertheless, I, the Lord, show it by vision unto many,
   but straightway shut it up again;
⁴⁸wherefore, the end, the width, the height, the depth,
   and the misery thereof,
   they understand not,
   neither any man except those
   who are ordained unto this condemnation.

NARRATOR:

⁴⁹And we heard the voice, saying:

THE LORD:

Write the vision,
   for lo, this is the end of the vision
   of the sufferings of the ungodly.

A VISION OF THE CELESTIAL KINGDOM

NARRATOR:

⁵⁰And again we bear record,
   for we saw and heard,
and this is the testimony of the gospel of Christ
   concerning them who shall come forth
   in the resurrection of the just:

THE LORD:

⁵¹They are they who received the testimony of Jesus,
   and believed on his name,
and were baptized after the manner of his burial,
   being buried in the water in his name,
   and this according to the commandment which he has given,
⁵²that by keeping the commandments
   they might be washed and cleansed from all their sins
and receive the Holy Spirit
   by the laying on of the hands
   of him who is ordained and sealed unto this power,
⁵³and who overcome by faith
   and are sealed by the Holy Spirit of promise,
which the Father sheds forth
   upon all those who are just and true.
⁵⁴They are they who are the church of the Firstborn;
⁵⁵   they are they into whose hands the Father has given all things;
⁵⁶they are they who are priests and kings,
   who have received of his fulness and of his glory
⁵⁷and are priests of the Most High,
   after the order of Melchizedek,
which was after the order of Enoch,
   which was after the order of the Only Begotten Son;
⁵⁸wherefore, as it is written,
   they are gods,
   even the sons of God;
⁵⁹wherefore, all things are theirs,
   whether life or death,
   or things present,
   or things to come.
all are theirs,

and they are Christ's,
and Christ is God's,
⁶⁰ and they shall overcome all things.
⁶¹Wherefore, let no man glory in man,
but rather let him glory in God,
who shall subdue all enemies under his feet.
⁶²These shall dwell in the presence of God and his Christ
forever and ever.
⁶³These are they whom he shall bring with him
when he shall come in the clouds of heaven
to reign on the earth over his people.
⁶⁴These are they who shall have part in the first resurrection;
⁶⁵ these are they who shall come forth in the resurrection of the just.
⁶⁶These are they who are come unto Mount Zion,
and unto the city of the living God,
the heavenly place,
the holiest of all.
⁶⁷These are they who have come to an innumerable company of angels,
to the general assembly and church of Enoch
and of the Firstborn.
⁶⁸These are they whose names are written in heaven,
where God and Christ are the judge of all.
⁶⁹These are they who are just men made perfect
through Jesus, the mediator of the new covenant,
Who wrought out this perfect atonement
through the shedding of his own blood.
⁷⁰These are they whose bodies are celestial,
whose glory is that of the sun,
even the glory of God,
the highest of all,
whose glory the sun of the firmament
is written of as being typical.

A Vision of the Terrestrial Kingdom

NARRATOR:

⁷¹And again, we saw the terrestrial world:

THE LORD:

And behold and lo,
   these are they who are of the terrestrial,
whose glory differs from that of the church of the Firstborn,
   who have received the fulness of the Father,
   even as that of the moon differs from the sun in the firmament.
72 Behold, these are they who died without law;
73   and also they who are the spirits of men kept in prison,
whom the Son visited
   and preached the gospel unto them,
   that they might be judged according to men in the flesh;
74 who received not the testimony of Jesus in the flesh,
   but afterwards received it.
75 These are they who are honorable men of the earth
   who were blinded by the craftiness of men.
76 These are they who receive of his glory,
   but not of his fulness.
77 These are they who receive of the presence of the Son,
   but not of the fulness of the Father.
78 Wherefore, they are bodies terrestrial,
   and not bodies celestial,
   and differ in glory as the moon differs from the sun.
79 These are they who are not valiant in the testimony of Jesus;
   wherefore, they obtain not the crown over the kingdom of our God.

NARRATOR:

80 And now this is the end of the vision which we saw of the terrestrial,
   that the Lord commanded us to write
   while we were yet in the Spirit.

A VISION OF THE TELESTIAL KINGDOM

81 And again, we saw the glory of the telestial,
   which glory is that of the lesser,
   even as the glory of the stars differs
   from that of the glory of the moon in the firmament:

THE LORD:

⁸²These are they who received not the gospel of Christ,
  neither the testimony of Jesus.
⁸³These are they who deny not the Holy Spirit;
⁸⁴ these are they who are thrust down to hell.
⁸⁵These are they who shall not be redeemed from the devil
  until the last resurrection,
until the Lord,
  even Christ the Lamb,
  shall have finished his work.
⁸⁶These are they who receive not of his fulness in the eternal world,
  but of the Holy Spirit through the ministration of the terrestrial;
⁸⁷ (and the terrestrial through the ministration of the celestial;)
⁸⁸and also the telestial receive it of the administering of angels
  who are appointed to minister for them,
or who are appointed to be ministering spirits for them;
  for they shall be heirs of salvation.

The kingdoms recapitulated

NARRATOR:

⁸⁹And thus we saw,
  in the heavenly vision,
the glory of the telestial,
  which surpasses all understanding;
⁹⁰and no man knows it,
  except him to whom God has revealed it;
⁹¹and thus we saw the glory of the terrestrial,
  which excels in all things the glory of the telestial,
  even in glory,
  and in power,
  and in might,
  and in dominion;
⁹²and thus we saw the glory of the celestial,
  which excels in all things,
where God, even the Father, reigns upon his throne forever and ever,
⁹³ before whose throne all things bow in humble reverence
  and give him glory forever and ever.
⁹⁴They who dwell in his presence are the church of the Firstborn;
  and they see as they are seen

Doctrine and Covenants 76

and know as they are known,
having received of his fulness and of his grace;
⁹⁵and he makes them equal in power,
and in might,
and in dominion.

The Kingdoms Again Recapitulated

⁹⁶And the glory of the celestial is one,
even as the glory of the sun is one;
⁹⁷and the glory of the terrestrial is one,
even as the glory of the moon is one;
⁹⁸and the glory of the telestial is one,
even as the glory of the stars is one;
for as one star differs from another star in glory,
even so differs one from another in glory in the telestial world;
⁹⁹for these are they who are of Paul,
and of Apollos,
and of Cephas;
¹⁰⁰these are they who say they are some of one and some of another,
some of Christ,
and some of John,
and some of Moses,
and some of Elias,
and some of Esaias,
and some of Isaiah,
and some of Enoch,
¹⁰¹but received not the gospel,
neither the testimony of Jesus,
neither the prophets,
neither the everlasting covenant.
¹⁰²Last of all, these all are they who will not be gathered with the saints
to be caught up unto the church of the Firstborn
and received into the cloud.
¹⁰³These are they who are liars,
and sorcerers,
and adulterers,
and whoremongers,

and whosoever loves and makes a lie.
¹⁰⁴These are they who suffer the wrath of God on earth;
¹⁰⁵ these are they who suffer the vengeance of eternal fire;
¹⁰⁶these are they who are cast down to hell
  and suffer the wrath of Almighty God
until the fulness of times,
  when Christ shall have subdued all enemies under his feet
  and shall have perfected his work;
¹⁰⁷when he shall deliver up the kingdom
  and present it unto the Father, spotless, saying,

THE LORD:

I have overcome and have trodden the wine-press alone,
  even the wine-press of the fierceness of the wrath
  of Almighty God.

NARRATOR:

¹⁰⁸Then shall he be crowned with the crown of his glory,
  to sit on the throne of his power
  to reign forever and ever.
¹⁰⁹But behold, and lo,
  we saw the glory and the inhabitants of the telestial world,
that they were as innumerable as the stars
  in the firmament of heaven,
  or as the sand upon the seashore;
¹¹⁰and heard the voice of the Lord saying:

THE LORD:

These all shall bow the knee,
  and every tongue shall confess
  to him who sits upon the throne forever and ever;
¹¹¹for they shall be judged according to their works,
  and every man shall receive according to his own works,
  his own dominion,
  in the mansions which are prepared;
¹¹²and they shall be servants of the Most High;
  but where God and Christ dwell they cannot come,
  worlds without end.

iii

Epilogue

NARRATOR:

¹¹³This is the end of the vision which we saw,
   which we were commanded to write
   while we were yet in the Spirit;
¹¹⁴but great and marvelous are the works of the Lord
   and the mysteries of his kingdom which he showed unto us,
which surpass all understanding in glory,
   and in might,
   and in dominion;
¹¹⁵which he commanded us we should not write
   while we were yet in the Spirit,
   and are not lawful for man to utter;
¹¹⁶neither is man capable to make them known,
   for they are only to be seen and understood
   by the power of the Holy Spirit,
which God bestows on those who love him
   and purify themselves before him;
¹¹⁷to whom he grants this privilege of seeing
   and knowing for themselves,
¹¹⁸   that through the power and manifestation of the Spirit,
   while in the flesh,
   they may be able to bear his presence in the world of glory;
¹¹⁹and to God and the Lamb be glory,
   and honor,
   and dominion,
   forever and ever.
Amen.

Commentary

The controlling themes of section 76 are stated in verses 5–7: the Lord will reward all men in eternity according to their faith in mortality, and his most faithful with eternal life and also with knowledge of hidden mysteries during this life. Although factual information about realms of existence that are usually hidden from mortals is contained in section 76, the main theme of the Lord's willingness to reveal his mysteries to his faithful in their mortality is equally important. As a matter of fact, little detailed information is imparted about life in the kingdoms of glory and in perdition; rather, the reader is invited to see for himself. The ladder of Jacob in Genesis 28:12 comes to mind: "And he dreamed, and behold a ladder set up on the earth, and the top of it reached to heaven: and behold the angels of God ascending and descending on it"; and Joseph Smith's comment on it: "Paul ascended into the third heavens, and he could understand the three principal rounds of Jacob's ladder—the telestial, the terrestrial, and the celestial glories or kingdoms, where Paul saw and heard things which were not lawful for him to utter" (*Teachings of the Prophet Joseph Smith*, p. 304).

Section 76 is rich in biblical allusion, but to spare tedium to the reader, who also can use a concordance, I cite only a (relatively) few key examples. Consider verse 19:

> and, while we meditated upon these things,
>   the Lord touched the eyes of our understandings,
> and they were opened,
>   and the glory of the Lord shone round about,

"The eyes of your understanding being enlightened" occurs in Ephesians 1:16-18, in the context of a prayer offered by Paul (rearranged in poetic form):

> Cease not to give thanks for you,
>   making mention of you in my prayers;
> That the God of our Lord Jesus Christ,
>   the Father of glory,
>   may give unto you the spirit of wisdom and revelation in the knowledge of him:
> The eyes of your understanding being enlightened;
>   that ye may know what is the hope of his calling,
>   and what the riches of the glory of his inheritance in the saints,

Section 76 thus is offered as a direct fulfillment of that prayer.

Consider the first words of the text: "Hear, O ye heavens, and give ear, O earth." They recall the first line of Isaiah, "Hear, O heavens, and give ear O earth," the only difference being the addition of "ye." The effect is immediately to connect the present work with the literary and prophetic traditions of the Bible, and particularly with the tradition represented by Isaiah, thus implying that what is about to be said is to be given the same weight as the words of Isaiah—a large claim, particularly in light of the observation by Christ himself in the Book of Mormon, "Great are the words of Isaiah" (3 Nephi 23:1).

A third example, verse 22: "And now, after the many testimonies which have been given of him, this is the testimony, last of all, which we give of him: That he lives!" "Last of all" recalls Paul's testimony of Christ in 1 Corinthians 15:8: "And last of all he was seen of me also."

Verse 23 is a recombination of biblical elements: "For we saw him, even on the right hand of God; and we heard the voice bearing record that he is the Only Begotten of the Father." "Saw him" occurs frequently in the Bible, but never in reference to Christ or God in heaven. "On the right hand of God" occurs several times in the New Testament, most pertinently in Acts 7: 55, 56, describing the vision of Stephen:

> But he, being full of the Holy Ghost, looked up stedfastly into heaven, and saw the glory of God, and Jesus standing on the right hand of God,
> And said, Behold, I see the heavens opened, and the Son of man standing on the right hand of God.

It is notable that in the larger context the author's testimony is ultimately followed by a martyrdom (see section 135), as is Stephen's in the immediate context.

Section 76 sometimes makes ironic use of biblical language by changing its intent. For example, returning to verse 1:

> Hear, O ye heavens,
>   and give ear, O earth,
>   and rejoice ye inhabitants thereof;

There is an important difference between what is about to follow the first two versets and what follows the similar language in Isaiah, for in Isaiah what follows is warning, and here we are given to know that there is cause for rejoicing. "Rejoice ye inhabitants thereof" vaguely echoes Biblical language, but with differences. Both the testaments contain directives to rejoice, but none directed to "ye inhabitants thereof." Furthermore, the present language is almost, though not quite, "the earth and all the inhabitants thereof," which occurs in Psalm 75:3, in, again, the context of judgment, not of rejoicing. "The earth, and the inhabitants thereof" occurs in Isaiah 40:22, in a context of comparing the greatness of God to the smallness of man; "inhabitants of the earth" occurs in Jeremiah 25:29 and 30, in the context of threatened punishment; in Daniel 4:35, comparing the power of God to the weakness of man; and in Revelation 17:2, in context with the "whore of Babylon"; whereas section 76 offers to the inhabitants of the earth the possibility of becoming as God is. Thus, the biblical language is given a new context and a new purpose, emphasized by contrast with the biblical use of the language, and an expectation is raised of a cause for rejoicing to be given in the subsequent text, an expectation that begins to be fulfilled in the very next words: "For the Lord is God, and beside him there is no Savior."

Another example, from verse 14, speaking of Christ: "Who is the Son, whom we saw and with whom we conversed in the heavenly vision." "Who is the son" occurs once in the Bible, in 1 Samuel 25:10, "And Nabal answered David's servants, and said, Who *is* David? and who *is* the son of Jesse?" Nabal asks the question about David rhetorically; in an ironic turn, this text uses the phrase positively to identify Christ.

Verse 17: "And shall come forth; they who have done good, in the resurrection of the just; and they who have done evil, in the resurrection of the unjust." This is a revised version of John 5:29, "And shall come forth; they that have done good, unto the resurrection of life; and they that have done evil, unto the resurrection of damnation." It was this difference that caused Joseph and Sydney to "marvel," as they say in the next verse: "Now this caused us to marvel, for it was given unto us of the Spirit." "Marvel" occurs in the Bible a number of times, as in Revelation 17:7: "And the angel said unto me, Wherefore didst thou marvel?" In this new context, however, a reason is given for marveling.

I end this sampling with verse 66:

> These are they who are come unto Mount Zion,
>   and unto the city of the living God,
>   the heavenly place,
>   the holiest of all.

"The holiest of all" alludes to Hebrews 9:3, 8: "And after the second veil, the tabernacle which is called the holiest of all. . . . The Holy Ghost this signifying, that the way into the holiest of all was not yet made manifest, while as the first tabernacle was yet standing." Section 76 makes plainer the way to "the holiest of all."

The text is organized by parallel structure at the most general level, as the themes of the prologue are recapitulated in the epilogue:

Prologue
A) Hear, O ye heavens,
and give ear, O earth,
and rejoice ye inhabitants thereof;
for the Lord is God,
and beside him there is no Savior.
B) Great is his wisdom,
marvelous are his ways,
and the extent of his doings none can find out.
His purposes fail not,
neither are there any who can stay his hand.
From eternity to eternity he is the same,
and his years never fail.

For thus saith the Lord:

C) I, the Lord, am merciful and gracious unto those who fear me
and delight to honor those who serve me
in righteousness and in truth unto the end.
Great shall be their reward,
and eternal shall be their glory,
D) and to them will I reveal all mysteries
yea, all the hidden mysteries of my kingdom from days of old;
and for ages to come will I make known unto them the good
    pleasure of my will
concerning all things pertaining to my kingdom.
Yea, even the wonders of eternity shall they know,
    and things to come will I show them,
    even the things of many generations,
and their wisdom shall be great
    and their understanding reach to heaven,
and before them the wisdom of the wise shall perish,
    and the understanding of the prudent shall come to naught;
for by my Spirit will I enlighten them,
and by my power will I make known unto them
the secrets of my will,

yea, even those things which eye has not seen,
nor ear heard,
nor yet entered into the heart of man.

Epilogue

A) This is the end of the vision which we saw,
   which we were commanded to write while we were yet in the Spirit.
B) but great and marvelous are the works of the Lord
   and the mysteries of his kingdom which he showed unto us,
   which surpass all understanding in glory,
   and in might,
   and in dominion;
   which he commanded us we should not write, while we were yet in the Spirit,
   and are not lawful for man to utter;
   neither is man capable to make them known,
C) for they are only to be seen and understood by the power of the Holy Spirit,
   which God bestows on those who love him
   and purify themselves before him;
D) to whom he grants this privilege of seeing and knowing for themselves,
   that through the power and manifestation of the Spirit, while in the flesh,
   they may be able to bear his presence in the world of glory.

Interlinear parallelism at a lower level and intralinear parallelism are also used to effect, but to avoid unnecessary tedium I point out here only some of particular interest. A classic sort of biblical parallelism is exemplified by the first line of the poem:

Hear, O ye heavens,
   and give ear, O earth,
   and rejoice ye inhabitants thereof;

The parallel versets move spatially from heaven, the address to which implies the cosmic implications of what is about to be delivered, downward to earth, and then to the inhabitants of the earth, progressively directing and focusing attention to the human addressees of the message to follow.

The next lines exhibit interlocking parallelisms:

> for the Lord is God,
>> and beside him there is no Savior.
> Great is his wisdom,
>> marvelous are his ways,
>> and the extent of his doings none can find out.
> His purposes fail not,
>> neither are there any who can stay his hand.
> From eternity to eternity he is the same,
>> and his years never fail.

The two versets of the first line are semantically parallel in a subtly complex way. "Savior" is a near-synonym of "God," and the line could appropriately have been written as "For the Lord is God, / beside him there is no God." The first verset tells us that the Lord is *the* God, not merely *a* God, and the second verset reinforces that assertion. The force of that assertion is not weakened by replacement of "God" with "Savior," but the verset adds incrementally to "God" by referring to one of God's roles, that of savior.

The second verset of the first line serves a dual parallelistic purpose: not only is it parallel to the previous verset, but it also forms the first element of an interlinear parallelism that continues through verse 4, describing the Lord who is God.

Verse 2 exhibits a freer sort of parallelism. The semantic parallelism in "great wisdom," "marvelous ways," and "extent of doings," is very general: they are all examples of the superlative nature of God.

Mankind is further directed to rejoice over what the Lord says, in the next stanza (verses 5–10):

> For thus saith the Lord:
>
> I, the Lord, am merciful and gracious unto those who fear me,
>> and delight to honor those who serve me
>> in righteousness and in truth unto the end.
> Great shall be their reward,
>> and eternal shall be their glory,
>> and to them will I reveal all mysteries,
>>> yea, all the hidden mysteries of my kingdom from days of old;
>> and for ages to come will I make known unto them the good pleasure of my will
>>> concerning all things pertaining to my kingdom.
> Yea, even the wonders of eternity shall they know,

>   and things to come will I show them,
>   even the things of many generations,
>   and their wisdom shall be great
>   and their understanding reach to heaven,
>   and before them the wisdom of the wise shall perish,
>   and the understanding of the prudent shall come to naught;
>   for by my Spirit will I enlighten them,
>   and by my power will I make known unto them the secrets of my will,
>   yea, even those things which eye has not seen,
>   nor ear heard,
>   nor yet entered into the heart of man.

The first line of this verse is parallel with with the second line of verse 1, both beginning coordinate clauses with the conjunction "for," under the main clause that is the first line of the poem. The basic organizing principle in these first three stanzas is this parallelism of coordinate clauses. The second and third stanzas are parallel in content as well as syntax, for they both give reasons for rejoicing. The latter intensifies the effect of the former by being set in the first person, as the words of the Lord himself, as against the third-person statement of the former. These relationships are obscured by the running text of the official edition, and also the punctuation, which leave the second "for," beginning verse 5, dangling without attachment to a main clause, and leaving the reader searching for one. A reader's first impulse is to connect it with the sentence immediately preceding— "From eternity to eternity he is the same, and his years never fail"—but the lines that follow do not logically function as an explanation of those words, as the word "for" indicates that they should; whereas it does logically perform that function in relation to the introductory lines. The first stanza thus introduces the subsequent two, as the whole of part i introduces the main body of the text—another parallelism in the text as a whole.

Verses 6–10 set forth the rewards to those who fear and serve God:

>   Great shall be their reward,
>   and eternal shall be their glory,

Verse 6 is a close syntactical parallelism.

> and to them will I reveal all mysteries,
>> yea, all the hidden mysteries of my kingdom from days of old;

The first line of verse 7 exemplifies a construction that is common in section 76. The first verset is not exactly parallel to the previous verset or line, but it picks up a word from the previous verset, "their," through a related pronoun, "them," and while maintaining that link advances the thought; and then the next verset of verse 7 picks up "mysteries" and expands on it, continuing the syntactic parallelism through the economy of ellipsis, "to them will I reveal" being only implied.

What happens next exemplifies a technique that is characteristic of section 76:

> and for ages to come will I make known unto them
>> the good pleasure of my will
>> concerning all things pertaining to my kingdom.

There is syntactic parallelism between that line and the first line of verse 7, between "to them will I reveal" and "will I make known unto them," and there is a certain semantic parallelism in the continuation of the enumeration of rewards to the faithful, even as the thought moves forward from "days of old" to "ages to come." Then, with the next verset, the poem leaps out of the box of classic biblical parallelism, while keeping a toe in touch with it. The second verset has no syntactic, and the barest semantic, parallelism with the first, but the word "all" connects it with the second verset of the previous line, which, of course, remains parallelistically linked with this next line. Through such chains, linked by a word, or an image, or a concept, section 76 advances thought rapidly while maintaining coherence through the merest gesture toward syntactic or semantic parallelism.

> Yea, even the wonders of eternity shall they know,
>> and things to come will I show them,
>> even the things of many generations,

The chain continues, "they" in the first verset linking with "them" of the previous line, "them" in the second verset linking with "they" of the first, "things" of the second verset with "things" of the previous line, "things" of the third verset with "things" of the second, and "of many generations" in the third verset making a semantic parallelism with "to come" of the second. Through that chain, temporal movement continues, from past to future, and now on into eternity. Then an odd thing happens: movement back from eternity to the mortal future. This seems rather anticlimactic, but it brings us us back to the present reality of mortality, where life must for the most part be lived, but with mindfulness that mortality is set against the backdrop of eternity, and in fact is a moment of eternity; and in the next line,

> And their wisdom shall be great
>   and their understanding reach to heaven,

which is an example of classic semantic parallelism, we are swept back toward eternity, with the second verset expanding "great" to "reach to heaven."

An interesting (and Whitmanesque) use of parallelism occurs toward the end of section 76, referring to sectarian ministers who find their final rest in the telestial kingdom:

> for these are they who are of Paul,
>   and of Apollos,
>   and of Cephas;
> these are they who say they are some of one and some of another,
>   some of Christ,
>   and some of John,
>   and some of Moses,
>   and some of Elias,
>   and some of Esaias,
>   and some of Isaiah,
>   and some of Enoch,
> but received not the gospel,
>   neither the testimony of Jesus,
>   neither the prophets,
>   neither the everlasting covenant.

These verses again hark back to the language of 1 Corinthians 15:40-41, but with a lengthening of the list of names, that greater length together with the abruptness of the versets in 99–100 emphasizing the fragmentation of the modern sectarian world.

In verse 7, the first verset of the second line

> And for ages to come will I make known unto them the good
>   pleasure of my will

is the longest in all three stanzas of the introduction, and one of the longest in the entire work. That verbal amplitude is expressive of the vast reach of the knowledge that the Lord offers.

The same device of a relatively long verset following a shorter one is used in this in this line to a different purpose:

> His purposes fail not,
>   neither are there any who can stay his hand;

There the comparative lengthiness of the line is analogous to the advance of an unstayed hand.

The opposite relationship, the following of a longer line by a shorter one, is used to effect in section 76.

> From eternity to eternity he is the same,
> and his years never fail;

The contrast of this short verset in comparison to the previous two longer closing versets gives it emphasis, a rhetorical "punch."

Section 76 is most interesting for its structure, however. It is something like a dramatic script for three actors, perhaps for a readers' theater. Two of the actors, or readers, standing visibly on an imaginary stage, are mortal humans called, respectively, "Joseph Smith Jr." and "Sydney Rigdon." The third, "the Lord," is not seen, but his voice is heard. "Joseph Smith Jr." speaks for himself and "Sydney Rigdon," introducing and concluding the presentation, reporting in brief summary certain visions seen by him and "Sydney Rigdon," and cueing "the Lord," who comments on the visions and their meaning. I have designated the speeches accordingly in my formatting of the text.

The text is divisible into a prologue, a main body organized thematically, and an epilogue; and those main divisions are further divisible. That organization is not arbitrary. The introductory verses, particularly 1–10, emphasize the Lord's desire and willingness to reveal to his faithful servants the things of eternity. The second part (verses 11–112) treats of some of those eternal things in descriptions of the glorified Lord and of the differing states to which human beings will arrive as the consequence of choices made during the mortal probation. The third part (verses 113 through 119) returns to the matter of the first, the Lord's desire and willingness to reveal his secrets to the faithful. By its placement immediately after the description of the glorified Lord and immediately before a description of the celestial glory, the description of perdition (verses 25–49) stands as a dark background against which the brightness of the kingdoms of glory is set. For another example, a symmetry in the descriptions of the kingdoms is achieved by the long description of the telestial glory in verses 99 through 112 set against the long description of the celestial glory in part 2, stanza 3. One of the most interesting structural features of the text is the recapitulations of the kingdoms of glory in verses 50–112. Verses 50–88 describe, in order, the celestial, the terrestrial, and the telestial glories. The kingdoms are then discussed in reverse order—telestial, terrestrial, and celestial, in verses 89–95. Then, in 96–98, they are briefly recapitulated again, in the original order of celestial, terrestrial, and telestial. Through the overall structure of the text, the reader is led three times, down and up and down again, to contemplate the descriptions of the kingdoms. The reader is invited to join Jacob and Paul, and Joseph and Sydney, in going up and down the "ladder."

The entire text of section 76 is comprises a single, over-all chiasm (designated "Chiasm 1"), as outlined here:

>Level 4 (1–24): Extended prologue (thematically parallel to epilogue)
>>Level 3 (25–49): The fate of the devil and the sons of perdition
>>>Level 2 (50–88): Enumeration of the degrees of glory
>>>>Level 1 (89–95): Enumeration of the degrees of glory in reverse order
>>>Level 2 (96–112): Enumeration of the degrees of glory in original order
>>Level 3 absent
>Level 4: (113–119): Epilogue (thematically parallel to extended prologue)

Note that there is no ascending level 3, concerning the devil and the sons of perdition. This not a flaw in the symmetry of structure, but rather an expressive variation, for the sons of perdition are lost and forgotten.

Doctrine and Covenants 76

Within that chiasmic whole are imbedded at least fifteen other chiasms, some within chiasms, some overlapping with other chiasms. Those sixteen chiasms are set forth here:

Chiasm 1 (verses 1–119)
Center element (verses 89–95): the three degrees of glory

Chiasm 2 (verses 3–4)
Center element (in verses 3–4): "neither are there any who can stay his hand; from eternity to eternity he is the same"

Chiasm 3 (verses 5–10)
Center element (verse 7): "to them will I reveal all mysteries")

Chiasm 4 (verse 7)
Center element (in verse 7): ("from days of old, and for ages to come"

Chiasm 5 (verses 11–27)
Center element (verses 15–22) "resurrection of the just . . . resurrection of the unjust" (John 5:17)

Chiasm 6 (verse 13)
Center element (in verse 13): "through his only begotten Son"

Chiasm 7 (verse 24)
Center element (in verses 24): "the worlds are and were created, and the inhabitants thereof" (by the Son)

Chiasm 8 (verse 27)
Center element (in verse 27): "[Lucifer] is fallen"

Chiasm 9 (verses 28–31)
Center element (in verses 28–29): Satan makes war against the kingdom of God and the Saints

Chiasm 10 (verses 32–38)
Center element (in verses 34–35): no forgiveness for sons of perdition

Chiasm 11 (verses 36–44)
Center element (verse 40): "this is the gospel"

Chiasm 12 (verses 45–49)
Center element (in verse 46): only sons of perdition and those to whom it is revealed know their fate

Chiasm 13 (verses 50–65)
Center element (in verses 54–59): glory of the members of the church of the Firstborn

Chiasm 14 (verses 63–107)
Center element (verses 80–81): end of the vision of the terrestrial glory

Chiasm 15 (verses 89–112)
Center element (verses 92–96): the celestial glory

Chiasm 16 (verses 113–119)
Center element (in verse 116): eternal things "are only to be seen and understood by the power of the Holy Spirit"

Especially noteworthy are chiasm 13 (verses 50–95) and chiasm 16 (verses 89–112), each enumerating, in opposite order, the degrees of glory, and overlapping in verses 89–95, which is itself an enumeration of the degrees of glory and which has been identified as the center element of the chiasmic whole. Verses 89–95 thus serve triply, as the center of one chiasm, the second half of another, and the first half of another. This arrangement calls for great concentration on that center enumeration of the degrees of glory. There are further complications to 13 and 16, however—two other, overlapping, chiasms are embedded within them: verses 50–65, regarding the inheritors of the celestial glory, comprise a four-level chiasm 14 (with its center element defining the church of the Firstborn), which overlaps with a four-level chiasm 15 (with its center element regarding the two lower kingdoms) comprised by verses 63–112, which is the final summary of all the degrees of glory and which contains the center of the chiasmic whole (verses 89–95).

That center is the fulcrum of section 76. Having solemnly marched deep into eternity to a vision of the glories, we are marched solemnly back out to the starting point (with the fresh view of the terrain that is offered by the parallelistic counterpoint of the corresponding elements), finding rest in the doxology that is the last verse. Section 93, to employ a musical metaphor, is a sonata; section 76 is a grand and complex fugue.

Doctrine and Covenants 88:1–68

NARRATOR:

¹Verily, thus saith the Lord
  unto you who have assembled yourselves together
  to receive his will concerning you:

THE LORD:

²Behold, this is pleasing unto your Lord,
  and the angels rejoice over you.
The alms of your prayers have come up
  into the ears of the Lord of Sabaoth
and are recorded in the book of the names of the sanctified,
  even them of the celestial world.
³Wherefore, I now send upon you another Comforter,
  even upon you my friends,
that it may abide in your hearts,
  even the Holy Spirit of promise;
which other Comforter is the same that I promised unto my disciples,
  as is recorded in the testimony of John.
⁴This Comforter is the promise which I give unto you of eternal life,
  even the glory of the celestial kingdom;
⁵which glory is that of the church of the Firstborn,
  even of God,
  the holiest of all,
through Jesus Christ his Son—
⁶ he that ascended up on high,

as also he descended below all things,
in that he comprehended all things,
    that he might be in all and through all things,
    the light of truth;
7which truth shineth
    (this is the light of Christ);
as also he is in the sun,
    and the light of the sun,
    and the power thereof by which it was made;
8as also he is in the moon,
    and is the light of the moon,
    and the power thereof by which it was made;
9as also the light of the stars,
    and the power thereof by which they were made;
10and the earth also,
    and the power thereof,
    even the earth upon which you stand.
11And the light which shineth,
    which giveth you light,
is through him who enlighteneth your eyes,
    which is the same light that quickeneth your understandings;
12which light proceedeth forth from the presence of God
    to fill the immensity of space—
13the light which is in all things,
    which giveth life to all things,
    which is the law by which all things are governed,
even the power of God who sitteth upon his throne,
    who is in the bosom of eternity,
    who is in the midst of all things.

14Now, verily I say unto you,
    that through the redemption which is made for you
    is brought to pass the resurrection from the dead;
15and the spirit and the body are the soul of man,
16   and the resurrection from the dead is the redemption of the soul;
17and the redemption of the soul is through him
    that quickeneth all things,
    in whose bosom it is decreed
    that the poor and the meek of the earth shall inherit it.

18Therefore, it must needs be sanctified from all unrighteousness,
    that it may be prepared for the celestial glory;

¹⁹for, after it hath filled the measure of its creation,
 it shall be crowned with glory,
 even with the presence of God the Father;
²⁰that bodies who are of the celestial kingdom
 may possess it forever and ever;
 for, for this intent was it made and created,
 and for this intent are they sanctified;
²¹and they who are not sanctified through the law
 which I have given unto you,
 even the law of Christ,
must inherit another kingdom,
 even that of a terrestrial kingdom,
 or that of a telestial kingdom;
²²for he who is not able to abide the law of a celestial kingdom
 cannot abide a celestial glory;
²³and he who cannot abide the law of a terrestrial kingdom
 cannot abide a terrestrial glory;
²⁴and he who cannot abide the law of a telestial kingdom
 cannot abide a telestial glory;
therefore he is not meet for a kingdom of glory;
 therefore he must abide a kingdom
 which is not a kingdom of glory.

²⁵And again, verily I say unto you,
 the earth abideth the law of a celestial kingdom,
for it filleth the measure of its creation,
 and transgresseth not the law;
²⁶wherefore, it shall be sanctified;
 yea, notwithstanding it shall die,
 it shall be quickened again,
and shall abide the power by which it is quickened,
 and the righteous shall inherit it;
²⁷for, notwithstanding they die,
 they also shall rise again,
 a spiritual body.
²⁸They who are of a celestial spirit
 shall receive the same body which was a natural body;
even ye shall receive your bodies,
 and your glory shall be that glory
 by which your bodies are quickened.
²⁹Ye who are quickened by a portion of the celestial glory

shall then receive of the same,
   even a fulness;
³⁰and they who are quickened by a portion of the terrestrial glory
   shall then receive of the same,
   even a fulness;
³¹and also they who are quickened by a portion of the telestial glory
   shall then receive of the same,
   even a fulness;
³²and they who remain shall also be quickened;
   nevertheless, they shall return again to their own place,
to enjoy that which they are willing to receive,
   because they were not willing to enjoy
   that which they might have received.
³³For what doth it profit a man if a gift is bestowed upon him,
   and he receive not the gift?
Behold, he rejoices not in that which is given unto him,
   neither rejoices in him who is the giver of the gift.

³⁴And again, verily I say unto you,
   that which is governed by law is also preserved by law,
   and perfected and sanctified by the same.
³⁵That which breaketh a law,
   and abideth not by law,
but seeketh to become a law unto itself,
   and willeth to abide in sin,
   and altogether abideth in sin,
cannot be sanctified by law,
   neither by mercy, justice, nor judgment;
   therefore, they must remain filthy still.

³⁶All kingdoms have a law given;
³⁷   and there are many kingdoms;
for there is no space in the which there is no kingdom;
   and there is no kingdom in which there is no space,
   either a greater or a lesser kingdom.
³⁸And unto every kingdom is given a law,
   and unto every law there are certain bounds also and conditions;
³⁹   all beings who abide not in those conditions are not justified.
⁴⁰For intelligence cleaveth unto intelligence;
   wisdom receiveth wisdom;
   truth embraceth truth;
   virtue loveth virtue;

light cleaveth unto light;
mercy hath compassion on mercy and claimeth her own;
justice continueth its course and claimeth its own;
judgment goeth before the face of him
who sitteth upon the throne
and governeth and executeth all things.
⁴¹He comprehendeth all things,
and all things are before him,
and all things are round about him;
and he is above all things,
and in all things,
and is through all things,
and is round about all things;
and all things are by him,
and of him,
even God,
forever and ever.

⁴²And again, verily I say unto you,
he hath given a law unto all things,
by which they move in their times and their seasons;
⁴³and their courses are fixed,
even the courses of the heavens and the earth,
which comprehend the earth and all the planets;
⁴⁴and they give light to each other
in their times and in their seasons,
in their minutes,
in their hours,
in their days,
in their weeks,
in their months,
in their years—
all these are one year with God,
but not with man.
⁴⁵The earth rolls upon her wings,
and the sun giveth his light by day,
and the moon giveth her light by night,
and the stars also give their light,
as they roll upon their wings in their glory,
in the midst of the power of God.

⁴⁶Unto what shall I liken these kingdoms,

that ye may understand?
⁴⁷Behold, all these are kingdoms,
and any man who hath seen any or the least of these
hath seen God moving in his majesty and power.
⁴⁸I say unto you, he hath seen him;
nevertheless, he who came unto his own was not comprehended.
⁴⁹The light shineth in darkness,
and the darkness comprehendeth it not;
nevertheless, the day shall come
when you shall comprehend even God,
being quickened in him and by him.
⁵⁰Then shall ye know that ye have seen me,
that I am,
and that I am the true light that is in you,
and that you are in me;
otherwise ye could not abound.
⁵¹Behold, I will liken these kingdoms unto a man having a field,
and he sent forth his servants into the field to dig in the field;
⁵²and he said unto the first,
"Go ye and labor in the field,
and in the first hour I will come unto you,
and ye shall behold the joy of my countenance";
⁵³and he said unto the second,
"Go ye also into the field,
and in the second hour I will visit you
with the joy of my countenance";
⁵⁴and also unto the third, saying,
"I will visit you";
⁵⁵and unto the fourth,
and so on unto the twelfth.
⁵⁶And the lord of the field went unto the first in the first hour,
and tarried with him all that hour,
and he was made glad with the light of the countenance of his lord.
⁵⁷And then he withdrew from the first
that he might visit the second also,
and the third,
and the fourth,
and so on unto the twelfth.
⁵⁸And thus they all received the light of the countenance of their lord,
every man in his hour,

and in his time,
and in his season,
⁵⁹beginning at the first,
and so on unto the last,
and from the last unto the first,
and from the first unto the last;
⁶⁰every man in his own order,
until his hour was finished,
even according as his lord had commanded him,
that his lord might be glorified in him,
and he in his lord,
that they all might be glorified.
⁶¹Therefore, unto this parable I will liken all these kingdoms,
and the inhabitants thereof,
every kingdom in its hour,
and in its time,
and in its season,
even according to the decree which God hath made.

⁶²And again, verily I say unto you, my friends,
I leave these sayings with you to ponder in your hearts,
with this commandment which I give unto you,
that ye shall call upon me while I am near.
⁶³Draw near unto me,
and I will draw near unto you;
seek me diligently,
and ye shall find me;
ask,
and ye shall receive;
knock,
and it shall be opened unto you.
⁶⁴Whatsoever ye ask the Father in my name,
it shall be given unto you,
that is expedient for you;
⁶⁵and, if ye ask anything that is not expedient for you,
it shall turn unto your condemnation.

⁶⁶Behold, that which you hear is as the voice
of one crying in the wilderness—
in the wilderness, because you cannot see him;
my voice, because my voice is Spirit.
My Spirit is truth,

truth abideth and hath no end,
   and if it be in you it shall abound;
⁶⁷and, if your eye be single to my glory,
   your whole bodies shall be filled with light,
and there shall be no darkness in you;
   and that body which is filled with light comprehendeth all things.
⁶⁸Therefore, sanctify yourselves
   that your minds become single to God,
and the days will come that you shall see him;
   for he will unveil his face unto you,
and it shall be in his own time,
   and in his own way,
   and according to his own will.

Commentary

Section 88 was given at Kirtland, Ohio, on the occasion of the return of missionaries from eastern cities in December 1832. The Kirtland Revelation Book divides it into two revelations, verses 1-126 having been given on December 27, the remainder on the following January 3. The first 126 verses may have been given in two sessions, as well, on two successive days. The Kirtland Council Minute Book records the circumstances as follows:

> A conference of High Priests assembled in the translating room in Kirtland Ohio on the 27 the day of Dec. A.D. 1832—Present—Joseph Smith,—Sidney Rigdon—Orson Hyde—Joseph Smith Jr.—Hyrum Smith—Samuel H. Smith—N.K. Whitney F.G. Williams—Ezra Thayer—& John Murdock commenced by prayer, Then Bro. Joseph arose and said, to receive revelation our minds on god and exercise faith and become of one heart and of one mind therefore he recommended all present to pray separately and vocally to the Lord for to receive his will unto us concerning the upbuilding of Zion, & for the benefit of the saints and for the duty and employment of the Elders—Accordingly we all bowed down before the Lord, after which each one arose and spoke in his turn his feelings, and determination to keep the commandments of God, And thus proceeded to receive a revelation concerning [not legible] above stated 9 oclock P.M. The revelation not being finished the conference adjourned till tomorrow morning 9 oclock

A.M.—27 met according adjournment and commenced by Prayer thus proceeded to receive the residue of the above revelation. . . .

The whole of section 88 can be read as a unified composition, but I have separated verses 1–68 from the remainder to point up the fact that they stand autonomously as a poem. I have not found it necessary to emend wording, although in the commentary I have supplied in brackets what seem to be elided words in order to make plainer some parallelisms.

Except for the brief introduction by a narrator, the entire text is spoken by the Lord. Thematically, section 88:1–68 is related to section 76, containing a review of the degrees of glory and promising the personal visitation of the Lord to the faithful individual. The central theme of this poem is the promise given in verse 68:

> Therefore, sanctify yourselves that your minds become single to God,
> and the days will come that you shall see him;
> for he will unveil his face unto you,

Again, the reader is invited to see the vision that has given rise to the poem.

Biblical language is used in this poem, but it is notable, particularly in its latter part, for new language that expands on the meaning of the old. The following are a few examples of each.

> Verily, thus saith the Lord unto you who have assembled yourselves together

"Assembled together" recalls Acts 4:31, "And when they had prayed, the place was shaken where they were assembled together; and they were all filled with the Holy Ghost, and they spake the word of God with boldness." The situations that call forth the spiritual outpouring are parallel.

> to receive his will concerning you:

"Will concerning you" recalls 1 Thessalonians 5:18, "In every thing give thanks: for this is the will of God in Christ Jesus concerning you."

By implication, the elders of this dispensation are identified with those of the previous one and are similarly blessed.

> Behold, this is pleasing unto your Lord,
> and the angels rejoice over you;

Two biblical passages are recalled: Colossians 3:20, "Children, obey your parents in all things: for this is well pleasing unto the Lord," and Luke 15:6–7,

> What man of you, having an hundred sheep, if he lose one of them, doth not leave the ninety and nine in the wilderness, and go after that which is lost, until he find it? I say unto you, that likewise joy shall be in heaven over one sinner that repenteth, more than over ninety and nine just persons, which need no repentance.

The implication is that the assembled brethren were considered in heaven as recovered lost sheep who have pleased their heavenly parent by their obedience.

> The alms of your prayers have come up
>
> into the ears of the Lord of Sabaoth,

"Come up into the ears of the Lord of Sabaoth" recalls language that is used in a very different context in James 5:4: "Behold, the hire of the labourers who have reaped down your fields, which is of you kept back by fraud, crieth: and the cries of them which have reaped are entered into the ears of the Lord of Sabaoth"—condemnation for injustice has turned to blessing for obedience.

Consider this line:

> and are recorded in the book of the names of the sanctified,
> even them of the celestial world.

The Bible contains nine references to a book in which the names of the saved are written, three in the Old Testament (as in Daniel 12:1, "And at that time thy people shall be delivered, every one that shall be written in the book") and six in the New Testament (as in Philippians 4:3, "my fellowlaborers, whose names are in the book of life"); the connection with "the celestial world" is new here.

Wherefore, I now send upon you another Comforter,

In the Gospel According to John, the Lord speaks of the Holy Ghost as "another comforter" (14:16, 26; 15:26; 16:7).

even upon you my friends,

The allusion is to Isaiah 41:8 ("the seed of Abraham my friend") and Luke 12:4 ("and I say unto you my friends").

That it may abide in your hearts,

"Abide" is common in the Bible, but "abide in the heart" is new.

even the Holy Spirit of promise;

"Holy Spirit of promise" occurs once in the Bible, in Ephesians 1:13, "ye were sealed with that holy Spirit of promise." A promise is here implied to the assembled high priests, which is amplified in the next words:

Which other Comforter is the same
that I promised unto my disciples,
as is recorded in the testimony of John.
This Comforter is the promise which I give unto you of eternal life,
even the glory of the celestial kingdom;

Continuing in section 88:

Which glory is that of the church of the Firstborn,

That lends meaning to "church of the firstborn" in Hebrews 12:23.

even of God,
the holiest of all,

"Holiest of all" occurs twice in Hebrews, but applied to a place in the tabernacle of Israel; application to God himself is new.

> Through Jesus Christ his Son—
>> he that ascended up on high,
>> as also he descended below all things,

"Descended" is common in the Bible, but the phrase above is new.

> In that he comprehended all things,

That is a new phrase.

> that he might be in all and through all things,

That is a new use of "in all things, and "through all things" is new.

> the light of truth;

That is a new phrase.

> Which truth shineth.

That is a new phrase.

> This is the light of Christ;

That is a new phrase, but the resonance with John 1:1–8 is unmistakable.

Cadence varies greatly. In places, as in the parable told in verses 51–61, it becomes "prosey," contributing to the relaxed mood. Many short parallel versets slow the reading, as in verses 44 and 48, contributing to the contemplative mood. The cadence of those verses is closely related to their syntactic parallelisms in lists of the kind that has already been noted in sections 93 and 76.

In general section 88 seems loose and flowing. Verset-to-verset parallelism almost entirely breaks down, but even the "prosiest" passages are structured by higher levels of parallelism, including chiasm. The text contains at least nine chiasms, as indicated here, with their center elements:

Chiasm 1 (verses 15): And the spirit and the body are the soul of man,
Chiasm 2 (verses 20–21): for this intent are they sanctified. And they

who are not sanctified through the law which I have given you, even the law of Christ, [must inherit another kingdom]

Chiasm 3 (verse 26): it [the earth] shall be quickened again and shall abide the power by which it is quickened, and the righteous shall inherit it.

Chiasm 4 (verse 37): [For there is no space] in the which there is no kingdom; and there is no kingdom [in which there is no space]

Chiasm 5 (verses 38–39): [unto every law] there are certain bounds also and conditions; all beings who abide not in those conditions [are not justified]

Chiasm 6 (verses 42–43): [he hath given a law unto all things, by which they move in their times and their seasons;] And their courses are fixed, even the courses of the heavens and the earth, which comprehend the earth and all the planets.

Chiasm 7 (verse 49): The light shineth in darkness, and the darkness comprehendeth it not;

Chiasm 8 (verse 59): from the last unto the first, [and from the first unto the last]

Chiasm 9 (verses 66–68): your whole bodies shall be filled with light, and there shall be no darkness in you; and that body which is filled with light comprehendeth all things.

Although section 88:1–68 is thematically related to section 76, its tone and mood are very different. Section 88:1–68 is to section 76 as Beethoven's Moonlight Sonata is to Handel's St. Matthew Passion. Where section 76 is grand and declamatory, the present work is hushed, meditative, a quiet reverie. Except for the brief introduction, the voice in section 88 is solely that of the Lord, who presents himself as tender, friendly, conversational. One thinks of the resurrected Lord breaking bread with the disciples who encountered him on the road to Emmaus, or even of the hinted domestic familiarity of the household of Lazarus, Mary, and Martha at Bethany. The gracious familiarity shows in the deceptive looseness, easiness, of the syntax and the deceptive wandering of the speech from topic to topic, as it develops organically, one thing leading conversationally to another. In verse 62, the Lord says, "I leave these sayings with you to ponder in your hearts." In verse 46, he sets an example, as he himself is presented as pondering how best to communicate his message; and there is irony in that verse, similar to that of section 93: "Unto what shall I liken these kingdoms, that ye may understand?" The Lord knows very well how best to speak to his servants; his gracious condescension is again emphasized by indirection here.

The most impressive moment in this poem is in the last words. Following the words that are the summary statement of the theme in verse 68 are these:

> And it shall be in his own time,
>   and in his own way,
>   and according to his own will.

The conclusion is abrupt but exquisitely tender and inviting, leaving the reader standing at a threshold in infinite expectation. It gives closure and unity to the deceptively wandering words that have preceded, acting as the fulcrum, like that of section 93, between what has been spoken and a pregnant silence; and here it is that section 88, like 93, fully comes to life as a poem.

Doctrine and Covenants 1

i

¹Hearken, O ye people of my church,
  saith the voice of him who dwells on high
  and whose eyes are upon all men.
Yea, verily I say: hearken ye people from afar,
  and ye that are upon the islands of the sea, listen together;
²for verily the voice of the Lord is unto all men,
  and there is none to escape,
and there is no eye that shall not see,
  neither ear that shall not hear,
  neither heart that shall not be penetrated;
³and the rebellious shall be pierced with much sorrow,
  for their iniquities shall be spoken upon the housetops,
  and their secret acts shall be revealed;
⁴and the voice of warning shall be unto all people,
  by the mouths of my disciples,
  whom I have chosen in these last days;
⁵and they shall go forth and none shall stay them,
  for I the Lord have commanded them.

ii

⁶Behold, this is mine authority,
  and the authority of my servants,
and my preface unto the book of my commandments,
  which I have given them to publish unto you,
  O inhabitants of the earth.
⁷Wherefore, fear and tremble, O ye people,

for what I the Lord have decreed in them shall be fulfilled;
⁸and verily I say unto you that,
   they who go forth bearing these tidings
   unto the inhabitants of the earth,
to them is power given to seal both on earth and in heaven,
   the unbelieving and rebellious;
⁹yea, verily, to seal them up
   unto the day when the wrath of God shall be poured out
   upon the wicked without measure,
¹⁰unto the day when the Lord shall come to recompense
     unto every man
   according to his work,
¹¹and measure to every man according to the measure
   which he has measured to his fellow man.

iii

Wherefore the voice of the Lord is unto the ends of the earth,
   that all that will hear may hear:

¹²Prepare ye, prepare ye for that which is to come,
   for the Lord is nigh;
¹³and the anger of the Lord is kindled,
   and his sword is bathed in heaven,
and it shall fall upon the inhabitants of the earth;
¹⁴   and the arm of the Lord shall be revealed;
and the day cometh that they who will not hear the voice of the Lord,
   neither the voice of his servants,
   neither give heed to the words of the prophets and apostles,
shall be cut off from among the people;
¹⁵   for they have strayed from mine ordinances
   and have broken mine everlasting covenant.
¹⁶They seek not the Lord to establish his righteousness,
   but every man walketh in his own way,
and after the image of his own god,
   whose image is in the likeness of the world,
and whose substance is that of an idol,
   which waxeth old and shall perish in Babylon,
   even Babylon the great, which shall fall.

iv

¹⁷Wherefore, I, the Lord,
    knowing the calamity which should come upon
    the inhabitants of the earth,
called upon my servant Joseph Smith Jun.,
    and spake unto him from heaven,
    and gave him commandments,
¹⁸and also gave commandments to others,
    that they should proclaim these things unto the world;
and all this that it might be fulfilled,
    which was written by the prophets:
¹⁹the weak things of the world shall come forth
    and break down the mighty and strong ones,
that man should not counsel his fellow man,
    neither trust in the arm of flesh;
²⁰but that every man might speak in the name of God the Lord,
    even the Savior of the world;
²¹that faith also might increase in the earth;
²²   that mine everlasting covenant might be established;
²³that the fulness of my gospel might be proclaimed
    by the weak and the simple
    unto the ends of the world,
    and before kings and rulers.

v

²⁴Behold, I am God and have spoken it;
    these commandments are of me
and were given unto my servants in their weakness,
    after the manner of their language,
    that they might come to understanding;
²⁵and inasmuch as they erred,
    it might be made known;
²⁶and inasmuch as they sought wisdom,
    they might be instructed;
²⁷and inasmuch as they sinned,
    they might be chastened,
    that they might repent,
²⁸and inasmuch as they were humble,

they might be made strong
and blessed from on high,
and receive knowledge from time to time;
²⁹and [that], after having received the record of the Nephites,
yea, even my servant Joseph Smith Jun.
might have power to translate,
through the mercy of God,
by the power of God,
the Book of Mormon;
³⁰and also that those to whom these commandments were given
might have power to lay the foundation of this church
and to bring it forth out of obscurity and out of darkness,
the only true and living church upon the face of the whole earth,
with which I, the Lord, am well pleased
(speaking unto the church collectively and not individually;
³¹ for I, the Lord, cannot look upon sin
with the least degree of allowance;
³²nevertheless, he that repents
and does the commandments of the Lord
shall be forgiven,
³³and he that repents not,
from him shall be taken even the light which he has received,
for my Spirit shall not always strive with man,
saith the Lord of Hosts).

vi

³⁴And again, verily I say unto you, O inhabitants of the earth:
I, the Lord, am willing to make these things known unto all flesh;
³⁵for I am no respecter of persons
and will that all men shall know that the day speedily cometh.
The hour is not yet,
but is nigh at hand,
when peace shall be taken from the earth
and the devil shall have power over his own dominion;
³⁶and also the Lord shall have power over his saints,
and shall reign in their midst,
and shall come down in judgment upon Idumea,
or the world.

vii

³⁷Search these commandments,
   for they are true and faithful,
   and the prophecies and promises which are in them
   shall all be fulfilled.
³⁸What I the Lord have spoken, I have spoken,
   and I excuse not myself;
and, though the heavens and the earth pass away,
   my word shall not pass away
   but shall all be fulfilled;
whether by mine own voice or by the voice of my servants,
   it is the same;
³⁹for behold and lo, the Lord is God,
   and the Spirit beareth record,
and the record is true,
   and the truth abideth forever and ever.

Amen.

Commentary

Joseph Smith presented the text of section 1 as a revelation given to him during a special conference of elders of the Church held at Hiram, Ohio, on November 1, 1831. One of the principal subjects addressed at that conference was the projected publication in book form, to be called the Book of Commandments, of revelations that had been received by the Prophet before that time. Circumstances prevented the publication of the Book of Commandments as such, but its purpose eventually was served by the Doctrine and Covenants. Quoting Steven C. Harper, "A committee drafted a preface for the book, but then, through Joseph, the Lord revealed his own preface, recorded now as Doctrine and Covenants 1" (*Making Sense of the Doctrine & Covenants: A Guided Tour through Modern Revelations*, p. 1). An often quoted record left by one William Kelly, who was present at the conference, describes the giving of that revelation in greater detail:

"A committee had been appointed to draft a preface, consisting of O. Cowdery and, I think Sydney Rigdon, but when they made their report . . . the conference then requested Joseph to enquire of the Lord about it, and he said that he would if the people would bow in prayer with him. This they did and Joseph prayed.

"When they arose, Joseph dictated by the Spirit the preface found in the Book of Doctrine and Covenants while sitting by a window of the room in which the conference was sitting; and Sidney Rigdon wrote it down. Joseph would deliver a few sentences and Sidney would write them down, then read them aloud, and if correct, then Joseph would proceed and deliver more, and by this process the preface was given" (quoted in Backman, *Joseph Smith and the Doctrine and Covenants*, 2).

The text represents the Lord as speaking to the people of all the earth and to the members of the Church in particular. The Lord describes it as "my preface unto the book of my commandments, which I have given them to publish unto you, O inhabitants of the earth" (verse 6). This section is often called "the Lord's preface" to the Doctrine and Covenants. The word "preface" is defined by a dictionary as "the introductory remarks of a speaker or author." A preface calls attention to points that the author wants the reader to bear in mind while reading a text.

As has been noted by other writers (see, for example, Harper, 20), this preface "frames" the Doctrine and Covenants in a typology of opposites: the type "Zion" and its antitype "Babylon." In Harper's words: "It separates mankind into two possible categories, the repentant and the unrepentant, and outlines the Lord's rationale for opening the last dispensation. The world was apostate, and the omniscient Lord has seen the devastating potential of such apostasy. He has provided a solution by calling a prophet, Joseph Smith, and giving him revelations, called 'commandments,' in section 1" (p. 19).

Consider the use of biblical language in the first lines of section 1:

> Hearken, O ye people of my church,
>   saith the voice of him who dwells on high
>   and whose eyes are upon all men.
> Yea, verily I say: hearken ye people from afar,
> and ye that are upon the islands of the sea, listen together;

These lines echo Acts 22:9, "voice of him"; Psalms 113:5, "the LORD our God, who dwelleth on high"; Jeremiah 16:17, "eyes are upon"; Is. 1:2, "Hear, O"; Psalm 65:5, "them that are afar off upon the sea"; Jeremiah 31:10, "in the isles afar off"; Isaiah 66:19, "to the isles afar off"; but the combination of those elements here is new. Furthermore, by opening with such words, so similar to Isaiah's opening words, "Hear, O heavens, and give ear, O earth," the text, like others, demands to be classed in the highest tradition of biblical prophecy, to be received with the utmost seriousness. The tenor of the whole section is such that this demand cannot be accidental.

Consider this:

> and the rebellious shall be pierced with much sorrow,
>   for their iniquities shall be spoken upon the housetops,
>   and their secret acts shall be revealed;

The Bible has "the rebellious" (e.g., Ezekiel 24:3) and "much sorrow" (Ecclesiastes 5:17), and "for their iniquities shall be spoken upon the housetops" recalls Luke 12:3, "that which ye have spoken in the ear in closets shall be proclaimed upon the housetops," and "their secret acts shall be revealed" more faintly recalls Psalms 90:8, "Thou hast set our iniquities before thee, our secret sins in the light of thy countenance," and all of the rest of the vocabulary of this line also is biblical, but the combination of elements is new.

> and the voice of warning shall be unto all people,
>   by the mouths of my disciples,
>   whom I have chosen in these last days;
> and they shall go forth and none shall stay them,
>   for I the Lord have commanded them.

"Voice" and "warning" and "unto all people" all are biblical, but not "voice of warning shall be unto all people"; this is a new combination of elements. "Go forth" is common, but not in context with words referring to the Lord's servants.

> Behold, this is mine authority,
>   and the authority of my servants,
>   and my preface unto the book of my commandments,
>   which I have given them to publish unto you,
>   O inhabitants of the earth.

In this line only the phrase "inhabitants of the earth" can be called biblical (see Jeremiah 25:9); the remainder of the language is new, but stylistically completely harmonious with biblical language.

> yea, verily, to seal them up
>> unto the day when the wrath of God shall be poured out
>> upon the wicked without measure,

That line recombines and concentrates several bits of biblical language: Ephesians 4:30, "whereby ye are sealed unto the day of redemption; Jeremiah 32:44, "and subscribe evidences, and seal them, and take witnesses; 2 Chronicles 34:25, "therefore my wrath shall be poured out; Isaiah 5:14, "hell hath enlarged herself, and opened her mouth without measure."

The very first line of section 1 illustrates the "free rhythm" that characterizes all these poems:

> Hearken, O ye people of my church,
>> saith the voice of him who dwells on high
>> and whose eyes are upon all men.

There is no "thought-rhyme" in that line; rather each subordinate verset further develops something that is set forth in the previous line. Despite this freedom, nevertheless, the versets make up a tightly controlled unit. The peremptory "voice" initially comes out of nowhere to capture attention; then, in the second verset, it is identified with God, who is localized on high; and in the third verset the more general idea of his being above us is sharply particularized and intensified: his eyes are upon us. The movement is from a disembodied voice, which startles us into looking about us, to God on high, to the very eyes of God.

Although the freer sort of parallelism is generally characteristic of this text, more typically biblical uses of parallelism are made. For example, the second line:

> Yea, verily I say: hearken ye people from afar,
>> and ye that are upon the islands of the sea, listen together;

The second verset semantically parallels the first, in calling upon people to hearken, but particularizes the call from those who are simply "afar" to those who are "upon the isles of the sea." Furthermore, the second line as a whole parallels the first in calling upon people to hearken, and also broadens its call, from the people of the Church to the whole world.

The next line continues the interlinear semantic parallelism, and within the line the second verset intensifies the first:

> for verily the voice of the Lord is unto all men,
>   and there is none to escape,

The next line

> and there is no eye that shall not see,
>   neither ear that shall not hear,
>   neither heart that shall not be penetrated.

continues the interlinear parallelism, reinforcing the fact of our inability to escape God and his warning; not only will he see us, he will get inside us: no one can escape seeing, hearing, and being penetrated to the very heart by his warning. There also is intensification within the line, from verset to verset, in the progression from seeing, to the more intrusive hearing, to the wholly intrusive penetration to the inmost being represented by the heart. Such biblical uses of parallelism are found throughout this text. Parallelism also is used in this text in a way that is quite unbiblical: that is, within long sentences that continue through many lines, as in the two-sentence second stanza. That stanza is notable for the swift, relatively unimpeded movement of thought and narrative.

Variation in parallelism and cadence is used effectively in this text. For example, consider verses 6–10. The lines in verses 9 and 10 are much longer than those that precede them; the very length of the lines in sudden contrast to the preceding ones conveys a sense of the "pouring out" of which they speak. An opposite effect is achieved by the very short versets in verses 24 through 29. Their "punchiness" lends emphasis to the Lord's determination to correct but in the end to sustain and justify his servants.

The structure of section 1 is perhaps the most complex of all these six poems, more so in certain respects than even section 76. Four principle general points work throughout the text:

1. All mankind, including the members of the Church, are called to hearken.
2. The world is in an apostate, wicked condition.

3. The world is warned of impending calamities as a consequence of its wickedness and is offered escape through repentance.

4. The Lord's servants who deliver his message speak with his authority, even in their personal weakness.

As indicated below, all four of the controlling themes are treated directly in each of the first four stanzas, and two or three in each of the last three stanzas, with variations in order, emphasis, wording, and development. It is on the basis of those groupings of ideas, in addition to the fact that each grouping of concepts begins with some kind of statement to the effect that the Lord has something to say, that I have distinguished the seven stanzas. The themes occur in the respective stanzas as follows:

Stanza 1: "Call to all mankind to hearken" (verses 1–2); "Warning," "Wickedness of the world" (verses 3–4); "Authority of the Lord's servants" (verse 5).

Stanza 2: "Authority of the Lord's servants," "Call to all mankind to hearken" (verses 6–7); "Authority of the Lord's servants even in weakness," "Call to all mankind to hearken," "Wickedness of the world" (verse 8); "Warning," "Wickedness of the world" (verses 9–10).

Stanza 3: "Call to all mankind to hearken" (verse 11); "Warning," "Authority of the Lord's servants" (verses 12–14); "Wickedness of the world" (verses 15–16).

Stanza 4: "Warning" (verse 17); "Authority of the Lord's servants," "Call to all mankind to hearken" (verses 17–18); "Warning" (verse 18); "Authority of the Lord's servants," "Warning," "Wickedness of the world," "Call to all mankind to hearken" (verses 19–23).

Stanza 5: "Authority of the Lord's servants" (verses 24–30); "Warning" (31–33).

Stanza 6: "Call to all mankind to hearken" (verses 34–35); "Warning" (verses 35-36); "Wickedness of the world" (verse 36).

Stanza 7: "Call to all mankind to hearken" (verse 37); "Warning" (37–38); "Authority of the Lord's servants" (verses 38–39).

The reader is led, as it were, to circle above the same territory seven times, attention being called to different features of the scene below and to different details of those features. Why all this repetition? For one thing, repetition is a teaching device. For another, it tells us by implication that these ideas are important—the speaker really wants them to register on us. Why seven times, not more or less? Possibly because seven is just enough to accomplish the speaker's purposes, for these repetitions are not as random in order or number as they may seem. They actually are carefully structured and modulated.

The first four paragraphs repeat all four of the basic ideas. Placing an item at the beginning or end of a paragraph gives it a special prominence, and each of the four ideas gets at least one of those prominent placements. The first and third paragraphs state each idea only once, for four statements; the second stanza states three of them twice, and one of them ("Warning") only once, for a total of seven statements. The fourth paragraph (the center paragraph, perhaps not accidentally) has a total of eight statements of idea, one of them ("Wickedness of the world") getting only one mention, but "Warning" getting three mentions. The extra semantic "weight" of the second and fourth paragraphs gives them a greater intensity, and the fourth has the greatest of all. There is therefore a rhythm of heightening intensity in these paragraphs—less, greater, less, much greater. Appropriately, considering the nature of the overall message, "Warning" gets doubly special prominence by being placed three times in the last of these four paragraphs. In addition, even in a stanza where a particular theme does not occur directly it is echoed by implication, while its absence allows for emphasis on others.

After repeating all four ideas with an over-all increasing intensity, the text in the fifth paragraph backs off two of them and gives the greatest prominence of all to one of them—"Authority of the Lord's servants, even in weakness"—devoting seven verses to it and "calling it out" by its placement in an abrupt change of pattern after the fourth paragraph, the speaker's thinking possibly being that the mortal weakness of the servants might be among the greatest obstacles to acceptance of the message, and then ends with a light note of "Warning," which, though it gets less emphasis at the moment, is not to be forgotten.

The last two paragraphs each recapitulate three of the four ideas, with final repetitions of "Call to all the world to hearken" and "Warning." "Wickedness of the world" and "Authority of the Lord's servants, even in weakness," get shorted on repetitions, but their prominent place at the ends of the paragraphs compensates. The final statement is one of support for the Lord's servants; despite their weakness, the message is true.

An interesting syntactical ambiguity exists in verses 17-23. What are the levels of subordination of the "that" clauses? I propose the following arrangement (and punctuate accordingly):

Wherefore, I, the Lord, knowing the calamity which should come
    upon the inhabitants of the earth,
called upon my servant Joseph Smith Jun.
and spake unto him from heaven and gave him commandments;
and also gave commandments to others,
that they should proclaim these things unto the world; and all this
that it might be fulfilled, which was written by the prophets:
    [that] the weak things of the world shall come forth and break
      down the mighty and strong ones,
    that man should not counsel his fellow man, neither trust in
      the arm of flesh, but
    that every man might speak in the name of God the Lord, even
      the Savior of the world;
    that faith also might increase in the earth;
    that mine everlasting covenant might be established;
    that the fulness of my gospel might be proclaimed by the weak
      and the simple
unto the ends of the world, and before kings and rulers

Chiasm figures prominently in section 1, with chiasms contained within chiasms, to at least four layers, and with chiasms overlapping with chiasms. The entire poem is a seven-element chiasm, as summarized below (relying heavily on King's analysis). Note that the center element affirms that "these are the Lord's commandments." Note also that the elements of that chiasm closely correspond to the stanzas into which I have divided the text, each stanza essentially containing one or two chiasms.

    7) verses 1–5: Voice of the Lord unto all people
      by the mouths of his disciples
      6) verses 6–7: All to be fulfilled
        5) verses 8–11: The Lord to recompense unto every man
          according to his works; the Lord is nigh
          4) verses 12–16: Those that heed not the words
            of the prophets and apostles to be cut off
            3) verses 17–18: Mission of Joseph Smith Jr. to proclaim
              commandments unto the world
              2) verses 19–23: Weak to proclaim
                everlasting covenant unto the ends of the world
                1) verse 24: These are the Lord's commandments

2) verses 24–28: Weak, humble, and repentant
      will be instructed
   3) verses 29–30: Mission of Joseph Smith Jr. to bring forth
      only true church
   4) verses 31–33: He that repents to be forgiven
   5) verses 34–36: Satan has power over own dominion;
      Lord has power over Saints; Lord is nigh
   6) verse 37: All to be fulfilled
   7) verses 38–39: Lord has spoken by his own voice
      or the voice of his servants

Two major divisions occur in the structure of the text, each of which is itself chiasmic. The first section comprises verses 1–16. The central theme of this chiasm, in verses 6 and 7, identifies this section as the Lord's preface to the Book of Commandments and affirms the certainty of the fulfillment of the prophecies it contains. The second major division, verses 17–39, has as its central theme the divine authority and power given to Joseph Smith to translate the Book of Mormon.

At the third level are chiasms 4 and 5. Chiasm 4 is wholly contained within chiasm 2, its central element again emphasizing that the "servants" have divine authority and that this section is the Lord's preface. Chiasm 5 overlaps with both 2 and 3, its central element emphasizing that these commandments are from heaven, given for certain purposes. Thus the center elements of all five of these first chiasms in one way or the other affirm divine authority for the Book of Commandments, and the interlocking of their formal structures reinforces that thematic relationship.

Contained within and interlocking with those first five chiasmic structures are eleven more, emphasizing, respectively, the universality of the target audience for section 1 (1), the universality of the target audience (1), the universality of the target audience (2–5), impending judgment (8–12), the disobedient state of the majority of mankind (13–16), divine authority for the message (17–18), purposes for which Section 1 is given (18–23), divine authority (24), forgiveness and condemnation for the repentant and the unrepentant, respectively (31–33), Lord and devil to rule over repentant and unrepentant, respectively (34–36), divine authority for section 1 (38–39). Thus the center elements of all the chiasms focus, in varying language, upon the four principle general points identified above as working throughout the text: (1) all mankind, including the members of the Church, are called to hearken;

(2) the world is in an apostate, wicked condition; (3) the world is warned of impending calamities as a consequence of its wickedness and is offered escape through repentance; and (4) the Lord's servants who deliver his message speak with his authority, even in their personal weakness—and all are framed within a single chiasm that drives home the point that the book that this section prefaces contains the Lord's commandments. Thus the device of chiasm is used to create an overall formal and a thematic unity and simultaneously to focus on several elements of that overall unity.

If section 1 is compared to a musical composition, it also, like section 76, plays out like a Baroque fugue, with four related themes winding through each other, reaching a climax of concentration in the fourth stanza, relaxing a bit in the fifth while one theme is brought to the fore, recapitulating in the sixth and seventh, and concluding crisply with the final notes: "and the record is true, and the truth abideth forever and ever. Amen." Or perhaps it is more like a jazz improvisation, with seven variations on a theme, or on combinations of themes. In fact, imagine two separate musical compositions, one the jazz improv, the other the fugue, such that, when the score of one is overlaid on the other, the individual notes turn out to be identical, the musical phrasing of the two in performance making all the difference.

The fulcrum of crossmotion in section 1 is the formal one of the level 1 element of the chiasm of the whole. An underlying tension permeates the whole, however, of the impending calamity against the compassionate concern of the God who must visit the final calamity upon his rebellious children. This is not the speech of a vengeful God who delights in unleashing his wrath on his creatures; rather, in the seven variant repetitions of his plea is revealed a loving, merciful God who ardently desires his children to turn from their disobedience in order to escape the inevitable consequences of rebellion. The words of Lehi come to mind: "Awake! and arise from the dust, and hear the words of a trembling parent" (1 Nephi 1:14).

Doctrine and Covenants 133

i

SPEECH I, THE LORD:

¹Hearken, O ye people of my church, saith the Lord your God,
    and hear the word of the Lord concerning you—
²the Lord who shall suddenly come to his temple;
    the Lord who shall come down upon the world
    with a curse to judgment;
yea, upon all the nations that forget God,
    and upon all the ungodly among you;
³for he shall make bare his holy arm in the eyes of all the nations,
    and all the ends of the earth shall see the salvation of their God.
⁴Wherefore, prepare ye,
    prepare ye, O my people;
    sanctify yourselves;
gather ye together, O ye people of my church,
    upon the land of Zion,
    all you that have not been commanded to tarry.
⁵Go ye out from Babylon;
    be ye clean that bear the vessels of the Lord.
⁶Call your solemn assemblies,
    and speak often one to another,
    and let every man call upon the name of the Lord.
⁷Yea, verily I say unto you again,
    the time has come when the voice of the Lord is unto you.
Go ye out of Babylon,
    gather ye out from among the nations,
    from the four winds,

from one end of heaven to the other.
⁸Send forth the elders of my church
   unto the nations which are afar off,
   unto the islands of the sea;
send forth unto foreign lands;
   call upon all nations,
first upon the Gentiles,
   and then upon the Jews.

⁹And behold, and lo, this shall be their cry,
   and the voice of the Lord unto all people:

SPEECH II, THE ELDERS:

Go ye forth unto the land of Zion,
   that the borders of my people may be enlarged,
   and that her stakes may be strengthened,
   and that Zion may go forth unto the regions round about.

SPEECH III, THE LORD:

¹⁰Yea, let the cry go forth among all people:

SPEECH IV, THE ELDERS:

Awake and arise and go forth to meet the Bridegroom;
   behold and lo, the Bridegroom cometh;
go ye out to meet him;
   prepare yourselves for the great day of the Lord.
¹¹Watch, therefore,
   for ye know neither the day nor the hour.
¹²Let them, therefore, who are among the Gentiles flee unto Zion,
¹³   and let them who be of Judah flee unto Jerusalem,
   unto the mountains of the Lord's house.
¹⁴Go ye out from among the nations,
   even from Babylon,
from the midst of wickedness,
   which is spiritual Babylon.

SPEECH V, THE LORD:

¹⁵But verily, thus saith the Lord:

Let not your flight be in haste,

Doctrine and Covenants 133

but let all things be prepared before you;
and he that goeth,
    let him not look back,
    lest sudden destruction shall come upon him.

ii

SPEECH VI, THE LORD:

¹⁶Hearken and hear, O ye inhabitants of the earth;
    listen, ye elders of my church together,
and hear the voice of the Lord;
    for he calleth upon all men,
    and he commandeth all men everywhere to repent.

¹⁷For behold, the Lord God hath sent forth the angel
    crying through the midst of heaven, saying:

SPEECH VII, THE ANGEL:

Prepare ye the way of the Lord,
    and make his paths straight;
for the hour of his coming is nigh,
¹⁸   when the Lamb shall stand upon Mount Zion,
and with him a hundred and forty-four thousand,
    having his Father's name written on their foreheads.
¹⁹Wherefore, prepare ye for the coming of the Bridegroom;
    go ye,
    go ye out to meet him.
²⁰For behold, he shall stand upon the mount of Olivet,
    and upon the mighty ocean,
    even the great deep,
and upon the islands of the sea,
    and upon the land of Zion.
²¹And he shall utter his voice out of Zion,
    and he shall speak from Jerusalem,
    and his voice shall be heard among all people;
²²and it shall be a voice as the voice of many waters,
    and as the voice of a great thunder,
which shall break down the mountains,
    and the valleys shall not be found.
²³He shall command the great deep,

and it shall be driven back into the north countries,
and the islands shall become one land;
²⁴and the land of Jerusalem and the land of Zion
shall be turned back into their own place,
and the earth shall be like as it was
in the days before it was divided.
²⁵And the Lord,
even the Savior,
shall stand in the midst of his people,
and shall reign over all flesh.
²⁶And they who are in the north countries
shall come in remembrance before the Lord,
and their prophets shall hear his voice,
and shall no longer stay themselves;
and they shall smite the rocks,
and the ice shall flow down at their presence,
²⁷ and an highway shall be cast up in the midst of the great deep.
²⁸Their enemies shall become a prey unto them,
²⁹ and in the barren deserts there shall come forth
pools of living water;
and the parched ground shall no longer be a thirsty land.
³⁰And they shall bring forth their rich treasures
unto the children of Ephraim, my servants,
³¹ and the boundaries of the everlasting hills
shall tremble at their presence.
³²And there shall they fall down and be crowned with glory,
even in Zion,
by the hands of the servants of the Lord,
even the children of Ephraim.
³³And they shall be filled with songs of everlasting joy;
³⁴ behold, this is the blessing of the everlasting God
upon the tribes of Israel,
and the richer blessing upon the head of Ephraim and his fellows;
³⁵and they also of the tribe of Judah,
after their pain,
shall be sanctified in holiness before the Lord,
to dwell in his presence day and night,
forever and ever.

iii

SPEECH VIII, THE LORD:

³⁶And now, verily saith the Lord:

That these things might be known among you,
   O inhabitants of the earth,
I have sent forth mine angel flying through the midst of heaven,
   having the everlasting gospel,
who hath appeared unto some and hath committed it unto man,
   who shall appear unto many that dwell on the earth;
³⁷and this gospel shall be preached unto every nation,
   and kindred,
   and tongue,
   and people;
³⁸and the servants of God shall go forth,
   saying with a loud voice:

SPEECH IX, THE SERVANTS OF GOD:

Fear God and give glory to him,
   for the hour of his judgment is come;
³⁹and worship him that made heaven,
   and earth,
   and the sea,
   and the fountains of waters;
⁴⁰calling upon the name of the Lord day and night,
   saying:

SPEECH X, THE LORD'S PEOPLE:

O that thou wouldst rend the heavens,
   that thou wouldst come down,
   that the mountains might flow down at thy presence!

SPEECH XI, THE LORD:

⁴¹And it shall be answered upon their heads,
   for the presence of the Lord shall be
   as the melting fire that burneth,
   and as the fire which causeth the waters to boil.

SPEECH XII, THE SERVANTS OF GOD:

⁴²O Lord, thou shalt come down
 to make thy name known to thine adversaries,
 and all nations shall tremble at thy presence—
⁴³when thou doest terrible things,
 things they look not for;
⁴⁴yea, when thou comest down,
 and the mountains flow down at thy presence.
Thou shalt meet him who rejoiceth and worketh righteousness,
 who remembereth thee in thy ways;
⁴⁵for since the beginning of the world have not men heard
 nor perceived by the ear,
 neither hath any eye seen, O God, besides thee,
 how great things thou hast prepared for him that waiteth for thee.

⁴⁶And it shall be said:

SPEECH XIII, THE PEOPLE OF THE WORLD:

Who is this that cometh down from God in heaven
 with dyed garments;
 yea, from the regions which are not known,
clothed in his glorious apparel,
 traveling in the greatness of his strength?

SPEECH XIV, THE SERVANTS OF GOD:

⁴⁷And he shall say:

SPEECH XV, THE LORD:

I am he who spake in righteousness,
 mighty to save.

SPEECH XVI, THE SERVANTS OF GOD:

⁴⁸And the Lord shall be red in his apparel,
 and his garments like him that treadeth in the wine-vat;
⁴⁹and so great shall be the glory of his presence
 that the sun shall hide his face in shame,
 and the moon shall withhold its light,
 and the stars shall be hurled from their places.

⁵⁰And his voice shall be heard:

SPEECH XVII, THE LORD:

I have trodden the wine-press alone
    and have brought judgment upon all people;
    and none were with me;
⁵¹and I have trampled them in my fury,
    and I did tread upon them in mine anger,
and their blood have I sprinkled upon my garments,
    and stained all my raiment;
    for this was the day of vengeance which was in my heart.

⁵²And now the year of my redeemed is come;
    and they shall mention the loving kindness of their Lord
and all that he has bestowed upon them according to his goodness
    and according to his loving kindness, forever and ever.
⁵³In all their afflictions he was afflicted.
    and the angel of his presence saved them;
and in his love,
    and in his pity,
he redeemed them,
    and bore them,
    and carried them
    all the days of old;
⁵⁴yea, and Enoch also,
    and they who were with him;
    the prophets who were before him;
and Noah also,
    and they who were before him;
and Moses also,
    and they who were before him;
⁵⁵and from Moses to Elijah,
    and from Elijah to John,
    who were with Christ in his resurrection.
And the holy apostles,
    with Abraham, Isaac, and Jacob,
    shall be in the presence of the Lamb;
⁵⁶and the graves of the saints shall be opened;
    and they shall come forth and stand on the right hand of the Lamb,
when he shall stand upon Mount Zion,
    and upon the holy city,
    the New Jerusalem;

and they shall sing the song of the Lamb,
    day and night forever and ever.

⁵⁷And for this cause,
    that men might be made partakers of the glories
    which were to be revealed,
the Lord sent forth the fulness of his gospel,
    his everlasting covenant,
    reasoning in plainness and simplicity—
⁵⁸to prepare the weak for those things which are coming on the earth,
    and for the Lord's errand in the day
    when the weak shall confound the wise,
    and the little one become a strong nation,
    and two shall put their tens of thousands to flight,
⁵⁹and by the weak things of the earth the Lord shall thrash the nations,
    by the power of his Spirit.
⁶⁰And for this cause these commandments were given;
    they were commanded to be kept from the world
    in the day that they were given,
    but now are to go forth unto all flesh—
⁶¹and this according to the mind and will of the Lord,
    who ruleth over all flesh.
⁶²And unto him that repenteth and sanctifieth himself before the Lord
    shall be given eternal life;
⁶³and upon them that hearken not to the voice of the Lord
    shall be fulfilled that which was written by the prophet Moses,
    that they should be cut off from among the people;

⁶⁴and also that which was written by the prophet Malachi:

SPEECH XVIII, MALACHI:

For, behold, the day cometh
    that shall burn as an oven,
    and all the proud,
        yea, and all that do wickedly,
        shall be stubble;
    and the day that cometh shall burn them up, saith the Lord of hosts,
        that it shall leave them neither root nor branch.

SPEECH XIX, THE LORD:

⁶⁵Wherefore, this shall be the answer of the Lord unto them:

⁶⁶In that day when I came unto mine own,
   no man among you received me,
   and you were driven out.
⁶⁷When I called again there was none of you to answer;
   yet my arm was not shortened at all that I could not redeem,
   neither my power to deliver.
⁶⁸Behold, at my rebuke I dry up the sea;
   I make the rivers a wilderness;
their fish stink
   and die for thirst;
⁶⁹I clothe the heavens with blackness
   and make sackcloth their covering;
⁷⁰and this shall ye have of my hand:
   ye shall lie down in sorrow.
⁷¹Behold, and lo, there are none to deliver you;
   for ye obeyed not my voice when I called to you out of the heavens;
ye believed not my servants,
   and, when they were sent unto you, ye received them not.
⁷²Wherefore, they sealed up the testimony and bound up the law,
   and ye were delivered over unto darkness.
⁷³These shall go away into outer darkness,
   where there is weeping,
   and wailing,
   and gnashing of teeth.

⁷⁴Behold, the Lord your God hath spoken it.

Amen.

Commentary

Section 133 was given at the same conference as section 1. It did not find its way into the Book of Commandments, but it was later included in the Doctrine and Covenants as the "appendix," thus framing that book along with section 1, the "preface" (Harper, p. 490).

Thematically, section 133 is similar to section 1: it contains the same typology of opposites in Zion and Babylon. The Lord is coming to judge mankind, his coming is to be preceded by calamities on Babylon, and all men are called to leave Babylon and find refuge in Zion.

As regards the use of Biblical language, the great achievement of this text is to recombine words and phrases of both the old and the new testaments to create a message of restoration, of the establishment of Zion in the New World ("the land of Zion" in speech ii is, historically, in Missouri), and of a gathering of Israel to that land. Particular uses of biblical language are also of interest. The opening words of both the first and second parts of section 133 echo those of section 1, thus demanding to be treated with the same gravity, and the opening lines of the third part iterate the sentiment, though not the exact words. The following line from part 1:

> Call your solemn assemblies,
>   and speak often one to another,
>   and let every man call upon the name of the Lord.

is particularly evocative in the context of this text, as the second verset recalls these words from Malachi:

> Then they that feared the Lord spake often one to another: and the Lord hearkened, and heard it, and a book of remembrance was written before him for them that feared the Lord, and that thought upon his name.
>
> And they shall be nine, saith the Lord of hosts, in that day when I make up my jewels; and I will spare them, as a man spareth his own son that serveth him.

Section 133 employs the same loose sort of interlinear parallelism as section 1. The versets vary in length between the long and the short, and a pattern is evident: information and expansive visions tend to be conveyed in more expansive lines, and commands tend to be given in short, peremptory lines that give them directness and force and make them difficult to misunderstand. This pattern is evident in the first speech, where the first four lines, conveying information and envisioning nations, the world, and the ends of the world are longer and are followed by a series of rather terse commands. Variation in length of versets is employed for emphasis in other ways, as well, as in these lines from speech ix:

> Behold, at my rebuke I dry up the sea.
> > I make the rivers a wilderness;
> > their fish stink,
> > > and die for thirst.

The short "Their fish stink," enhanced by the harsh final word, comes with blunt force after the longer, more euphonious previous two lines (and it so happens that they come at the center of a chiasm, giving them added emphasis).

The structure as well as the theme of section 133 is similar to that of section 1, in that the basic themes are presented repeatedly, in this case three times, in identifiable separate parts. Each of the three main parts (verses 1-15, verses 15-35, and verses 36-74) could stand as an autonomous unit, but they are related, not only by theme, but also formally: each part begins with a call to hearken, in the first a call to the people of the Church, in the second to the world at large and to the people of the Church, in the third to the world at large; the three calls thus interlock in a kind of symmetry.

Ten complete chiasms are discernible in section 133: verse 3; verses 4-5; verses 7-9; verse 10; verses 27-31; verses 36-37; verses 46-48; verses 52-53; verse 56; verses 63-74, as set forth here:

The central elements in these chiasms are, respectively: "all the nations / and all the ends of the earth" (specifying who shall see the returning Lord; verse 3); "go ye out from Babylon" (the directive to those who would be saved; verse 5); "call upon all nations, first upon the Gentiles, and then upon the Jews, And behold, and lo, this shall be their cry" (speaking of the elders; verses 8-9); "behold and lo, the Bridegroom cometh" (verse 10); "And in the barren deserts there shall come forth pools of living water, and the parched ground shall no longer be a thirsty land" (where those of the north countries pass through; verse 29); "I have sent forth mine angel flying through the midst of heaven" (verse 36); "greatness of his strength" (speaking of the returning Lord; verse 46); "I have trampled them in my fury" (spoken by the returning Lord; verse 51); "and according to his goodness, and according to his loving kindness" (spoken of the Lord by his redeemed; verse 52)—a good summary of the main points communicated by the several speakers in this section. It should be noted that one of these chiasms (46-48) covers four speeches.

Section 133 differs from section 1 in that the latter is spoken by a single voice, that of the Lord, whereas the former is like a script for a pageant or a readers' theater, with at least six different speakers of nineteen speeches. There is the Lord (referring to himself in the third person), the Lord as quoted by himself, an angel, servants of the Lord, elders, and the people of the world. The Lord serves as a kind of stage manager, cueing now one, now another of the other speakers. The number of the voices differs among the three main parts. The first contains two voices, the Lord and the elders, in five speeches. The second is the simplest of the three in this regard, with two voices, the Lord and the angel, and only two speeches—a long one by the angel, introduced by a much shorter one by the Lord. The third is the most complex of all, with five voices represented—the Lord, the servants of God, the Lord's people, the people of the world, Malachi—in eleven different speeches.

There is thus a rhythm of complexity, from an initial level, to a lower level, to the highest. If a theatrical presentation of this text is envisioned, with the spotlight shifting from one speaker to another, and perhaps with suitable accompanying music, then there is also a parallel rhythm of dramatic intensity. Having reached the highest intensity, the whole presentation is quickly and emphatically terminated by the final words: "Behold, the Lord God hath spoken it. Amen," in a manner similar to that of section 1. The overall tone of section 133 differs from that of section 1. It is more declamatory, more strident, more threatening, and simultaneously more celebratory of the Lord's return in glory: it is an enactment of celebration.

Doctrine and Covenants
121:1–25, 122:1–9

i

^{121:1}O GOD, where art thou?
   and where is the pavilion that covereth thy hiding place?
²How long shall thy hand be stayed,
   and thine eye—
   yea, thy pure eye—
behold from the eternal heavens the wrongs of thy people
   and of thy servants,
   and thine ear be penetrated with their cries?
³Yea, O Lord, how long shall they suffer these wrongs
   and unlawful oppressions,
     before thine heart shall be softened toward them
     and thy bowels be moved with compassion toward them?

⁴O Lord God Almighty,
   maker of heaven, earth, and seas
   and of all things that in them are,
and who controllest and subjectest the devil
   and the dark and benighted dominion of Sheol:
stretch forth thy hand,
   let thine eye pierce,
let thy pavilion be taken up,
   let thy hiding place no longer be covered,
let thine ear be inclined,
   let thine heart be softened
   and thy bowels moved with compassion toward us,

⁵let thine anger be kindled against our enemies,
   and, in the fury of thine heart,
   with thy sword avenge us of our wrongs.
⁶Remember thy suffering saints, O our God,
   and thy servants will rejoice in thy name forever.

ii

⁷MY SON, peace be unto thy soul;
   thine adversity and thine afflictions shall be but a small moment,
⁸and then, if thou endure it well,
   God shall exalt thee on high;
   thou shalt triumph over all thy foes.
⁹Thy friends do stand by thee,
   and they shall hail thee again,
   with warm hearts and friendly hands.
¹⁰Thou art not yet as Job:
   thy friends do not contend against thee,
   neither charge thee with transgression, as they did Job;
¹¹and they who do charge thee with transgression,
   their hope shall be blasted,
and their prospects shall melt away
   as the hoar frost melteth before the burning rays of the rising [sun.
¹²God] hath set his hand and seal
   to change the times and seasons
   and to blind their minds,
that they may not understand his marvelous workings;
   that he may prove them also
   and take them in their own craftiness;
¹³[also, that the things which they are willing to bring upon others
   and love to have others suffer,
   because their hearts are corrupted,]
   may come upon themselves to the very uttermost;
¹⁴that they may be disappointed also,
   and their hopes may be cut off;
¹⁵and, not many years hence,
   that they and their posterity shall be swept from under heaven,
   that not one of them is left to stand by the wall.
¹⁶Cursed are all those that shall lift up the heel against mine anointed
   and cry they have sinned when they have not sinned before me,

but have done that which was meet in mine eyes
    and which I commanded them;
17but those who cry transgression
    do it because they are the servants of sin
    and are the children of disobedience themselves;
18and those who swear falsely against my servants,
    that they might bring them into bondage and death—
19wo unto them because they have offended my little ones:
    they shall be severed from the ordinances of mine house.
20Their basket shall not be full,
    their houses and their barns shall perish,
    and they themselves shall be despised by those that flattered them.
21They shall not have right to the priesthood,
    nor their posterity after them from generation to generation.
22It had been better for them
    that a millstone had been hanged about their necks
    and they drowned in the depth of the sea.
23Wo unto all those that discomfort my people
    and drive, and murder, and testify against them.
A generation of vipers shall not escape the damnation of hell;
24   behold, mine eyes see and know all their works,
and I have in reserve a swift judgment,
    in the season thereof, for them all;
25For there is a time appointed for every man,
    according as his works shall be.

122:1The ends of the earth shall inquire after thy name,
    and fools shall have thee in derision,
    and hell shall rage against thee,
2while the pure in heart,
    and the wise,
    and the noble,
    and the virtuous,
shall seek counsel,
    and authority,
    and blessings
    constantly from under thy hand;
3and thy people shall never be turned against thee
    by the testimony of traitors;
4and, although their influence shall cast thee into trouble
    and into bars and walls,

thou shalt be held in honor;
  and, but for a small moment,
and thy voice shall be more terrible in the midst of thine enemies
      than the fierce lion
  because of thy righteousness;
and thy God shall stand by thee forever and ever.
5If thou art called to pass through tribulation,
if thou art in perils among false brethren,
if thou art in perils among robbers,
if thou art in perils by land or by sea,
6if thou art accused with all manner of false accusations,
if thine enemies fall upon thee,
if they tear thee from the society of thy father and mother
  and brethren and sisters,
and if with a drawn sword thine enemies tear thee
  from the bosom of thy wife
  and of thine offspring,
and thine elder son,
  although but six years of age,
shall cling to thy garments, and shall say,
    "My father, my father, why can't you stay with us?
    O, my father, what are the men going to do with you?"
and if then he shall be thrust from thee by the sword,
  and thou be dragged to prison,
  and thine enemies prowl around thee
  like wolves for the blood of the lamb,
7and if thou shouldst be cast into the pit
  or into the hands of murderers
  and the sentence of death passed upon thee,
if thou be cast into the deep,
if the billowing surge conspire against thee,
if fierce winds become thine enemy,
if the heavens gather blackness
  and all the elements combine to hedge up the way,
and, above all, if the very jaws of hell
  shall gape open the mouth wide after thee,
know thou, my son, that all these things shall give thee experience
  and shall be for thy good.
8The Son of Man hath descended below them all;
  art thou greater than he?

⁹Therefore, hold on thy way,
   and the priesthood shall remain with thee,
for their bounds are set;
   they cannot pass.
Thy days are known,
   and thy years shall not be numbered less.
Therefore, fear not what man can do,
   for God shall be with you forever and ever.

COMMENTARY

The original text of Doctrine and Covenants 121, 122, and 123 is found in a letter dictated by Joseph Smith to a fellow prisoner in Liberty Jail on March 20, 1839, as his people were making their way across northern Missouri toward Illinois under Governor Lilburn Boggs' extermination order. A typescript presentation of the handwritten letter from which the prayer and the Lord's answer are drawn can be found in *The Personal Writings of Joseph Smith*. The letter is addressed "To the church of Latter-day saints at Quincy Illinois and scattered abroad and to Bishop Partridge in particular," in care of Joseph's wife Emma.

Five passages from that letter, separated in the original by intervening text, have been published in the Doctrine and Covenants as sections 121, 122, and 123. It is evident from context and internal evidence that the third passage (now D&C 121:26–32), the fourth (now D&C 121:33), and the first half of the fifth (now D&C 121:34–46) are spoken as by the Prophet to his brethren. The first, now 121:1–6, is clearly a prayer addressed by Joseph to the Lord. It seems also clear that the second, now 121:7–25, is spoken by the Lord in answer to the prayer. The latter part of the fifth, now separated out as section 122, seems actually, thematically and stylistically, to be a continuation of the Lord's answer to Joseph's prayer.

Why these passages are arranged as they now are in the official edition of the Doctrine and Covenants, and whether they could or should be arranged there differently are questions beyond my purview; but what I am interested in here is what happens when the first, the second, and the latter part of the fifth are combined as I have done. What happens is a poem.

On the way to the final poem, as presented above, I have emended the original text and the current Doctrine and Covenants text in certain ways. Most of these emendations are to punctuation, bringing the text into line with modern practice. Three, however, are to wording. As Richard L. Bushman describes Joseph's process of composition of the letter in Liberty Jail, "the words came rapidly from his lips without calculated organization. No paragraphs break up the flow; sentences merge; frequent misplaced and misspelled words show the rush in which the dictation was scribbled down." Given the circumstances of the composition of the text from which this poem is drawn, it should not be surprising that either Joseph himself or his scribe occasionally lost the train of syntax. In fact, two problems of syntax occur in the original text and in the current Doctrine and Covenants versions of the passages under consideration. The first is in section 121, in verses 11 and 12:

> And they who do charge thee with transgression, their hope shall be blasted, and their prospects shall melt away as the hoar frost melteth before the burning rays of the rising sun;
> And also that God hath set his hand a seal to change the times and seasons, and to blind their minds, that they may not understand his marvelous workings; that he may prove them also and take them in their own craftiness;

The "that" clause in the second verse has no proper syntactical relationship to the surrounding text, and I have discovered no manipulation of punctuation that can give it one. Seeking the semantic intent, I have emended the wording as follows: " . . . as the hoar frost melteth before the burning rays of the rising sun. / God hath set his hand. . . ."

The syntax appears to lose its way again between verses 12 and 13:

> . . . that he may prove them also and take them in their own craftiness;
> Also because their hearts are corrupted, and the things which they are willing to bring upon others, and love to have others suffer, may come upon themselves to the very uttermost;

Again seeking the semantic intent, I have revised that wording as follows: " . . . and take them in their own craftiness; / also, that the things which they are willing to bring upon others and love to have others suffer, because their hearts are corrupted, may come upon themselves. . . ."

The two passages combined as I have presented them coalesce as a highly unified poem in a biblical mode. It is a bit of call-and-response dialogue, a brief drama of cosmic implications, whose characters are a supplicant and his God, with its clearest biblical precedent in the Book of Habakkuk.

The first speech, the supplicant's prayer, actually is capable of standing alone as a complete, unified poem The prayer itself is divided into two parts, the anguished plea for an explanation of God's staying of his hand, and the importuning of God to action. There is irony in this speech: the human mortal, mindful of the inadequacy of his own power to defend against his and his people's enemies, of his utter dependency on an all-knowing and all-powerful God, whose knowledge and power he fully acknowledges, cannot withhold himself from an implied reproach of that same God, revealed in the breathtaking audacity of the opening verset: "O God, where art thou?" "Where art thou?" occurs once in the Bible, in Genesis 3:9, where it is used by the Lord to call Adam out of hiding to account for his transgression and to expose Adam's shame. The gracious patience with which the Lord answers Joseph's question is perhaps the main significance of this poem.

There is a further irony, and considerable pathos, in the supplicant's attempt to bargain with this apparently unresponsive God, whom he acknowledges as already possessing, in fact as having made, all things, by making him the paltry offering of the praise of implicitly acknowledged inferiors. The formal unity of this prayer is reinforced by the use of the word "pavilion" in both sections and by judicious use of internal rhyme ("oppression . . . compassion") and alliteration ("sword . . . suffering saints . . . servants" to link key words.

The use of the word "pavilion" is of particular interest. A pavilion is a tent associated with warriors and knights. The supplicant is pleading with God to come out of his tent and act as a warrior, as, in the *Illiad*, Achilles is begged to come out of his tent and fight for the Achaeans.

But though the prayer can stand alone as a poem, it also functions as a component of a larger unit. The answer is a partial granting of what is requested in the prayer: God comes forth from hiding, not yet to act but to promise to act. The answer can be read as being directed solely to the supplicant, who in this case can hardly be separated in identity from the author himself, but the prayer is spoken on behalf of the supplicant's whole people, and the answer could as well have been directed to any one of the Saints who were struggling across Missouri leaving bloody footprints in the snow in March 1839, and indeed to anyone anywhere, at any time, who suffers severe persecution for service to his God.

The essence of the answer is summarized succinctly in the last two lines: "fear not what man can do, / for God shall be with you forever and ever"; but the answer is lengthy and nuanced. It begins with words of calm and reassurance: "My son, peace be unto thy soul." There is no condemnation of the supplicant for his doubts, his implied reproach of God, or the doubtfully Christian craving for vengeance; rather there is sympathy for the human plight and the human response to it. But there are then a few words of gentle reproach: "Thou art not yet as Job," implying that perhaps the supplicant has been indulging in some self pity in thinking of himself as Job, and reminding the supplicant that God's "pure eye" does in fact "pierce" into the deepest heart of the "righteous" as well as to that of the "wicked." There is, in historical hindsight, further irony in that reproach, because God does not say that, in fact, things might not yet get worse, as they in fact ultimately did, for both Joseph and his people, as they were betrayed by some of their own.

There then follows a long description of the judgments to be brought upon the persecutors, sufficient to satisfy the human longing for justice and revenge; and embedded in the list of judgments is another expression of tenderness for the persecuted Saints: God opens his answer with the words "my son"; then he refers to the Saints as "my little ones," and a few lines later he says of the persecutors that "it had been better for them that a millstone had been hanged about their necks, and they drowned in the depth of the sea," a judgment that is spoken elsewhere in scripture exclusively against those who offend those who are children in the literal sense. But in touching and again ironic counterpoint, God also speaks of the persecutors as "children," though as "children of disobedience," and this usage resonates with another passage from "the works of Joseph Smith," Moses 7:28–37, in which God is seen weeping for his disobedient children. That sorrow is not emphasized in this exchange with the supplicant—there is other, urgent business at hand at the moment—but the supplicant is obliquely reminded of it.

Parallelism, in combination with cadence, is used in this poem with particular effectiveness. Consider the first four lines of the prayer. In each line, each subordinate verset is a semantic elaboration of the preceding one, and there is a movement from the more general to the more concrete and specific, or from the less vivid imagery to the more vivid. The entire passage presents an intensification of language from "where art thou" to "thy bowels be moved by compassion." The first two lines achieve a peculiar intensity by setting the two brief versets of the second line against the ample second verset of the first line and by closely focusing attention on the striking image of the "eye— / yea, thy pure eye" of God; and then in dramatic contrast the subsequent lines roll forth in a release of dammed-up feeling. There is rhetorical force in the repetition of key phrases and words ("eye— / yea, thy pure eye" and "compassion toward them / softened toward them").

As the first part of the prayer is about feeling and intensification of feeling, the second part is about action and narrative, as the almighty God is envisioned as recognizing the plight of his people and rising to defend and avenge them. The first part is all pathetic and desperate plea; the second begins with an invocation of divine might and then erupts into the imperative and even peremptory: "Stretch forth thy hand; / let thine eye pierce," and proceeds through a swift narrative development.

The Lord's answer demonstrates the same combination of intensification and narrative development. An especially notable example of the latter is the long passage, verses 122:5–8, that begins with "If thou art called to pass through tribulation" and ends with "if the very jaws of hell shall gape open the mouth wide after thee"; and this narrative is intensified from the general "tribulation" through the pitiable pleas of the young son, to the gaping open of "the very jaws of hell." That also is an example of the Whitmanesque sort of "list" parallelism that has already been noted in these poems, and one of great rhetorical intensity, enhanced by the short, pounding versets. Joseph once spoke of "the visions that roll like an overflowing surge before my mind"; there are the roll and surge of a violent sea in the syntax and cadences of this poem.

The last line of the answer in a final parallelism echoes the last line of the prayer ("thy servants will rejoice in thy name forever"), but with emphasis ("and ever"), for God offers more in return for patience than the supplicant can offer for release and justice; and this echoing promise rounds off the formal unity of the whole.

Further Observations and Some Conclusions

Why poems, and why this particular kind of poem? Why does a prophet whose purpose is to turn his audience's attention to God and God's will and purposes employ a text that is, as a poem, as an "aesthetic object," by its nature intransitive—that is, a text so designed as to hold attention within itself, on its internal relationships? I submit in answer that the very fact that these texts are unified works of art has theological significance.

Before getting into that, however, it seems advisable to make fully explicit the theory of art that underlies this essay. I subscribe to a view that has its roots in Immanuel Kant and runs through Ernst Cassirer to a philosopher who was closely associated with the Anglo-American formalists of the twentieth century and who seems to have enjoyed a vogue among graduate students of the nineteen-fifties but whose name has vanished from the critical and theoretical conversation: Eliseo Vivas. There will be quarrel with this position, but the most superficial study of the history of aesthetic and critical thought discovers that there will be quarrel with any position. One must start somewhere, and I find this position convincing and serviceable.

"Man is the symbolizing animal," as Cassirer put it. We know through the mediation of symbols. The human mind does not receive the raw data of experience passively, but rather, actively "[organizes] the primary subject matter of experience" (Vivas, p. 117). The mind *constitutes* the world. This constitutive function is the aesthetic function. Quoting Vivas further:

> Knowledge, morality, and religion, presuppose and build on

the world we come to know by means of art. The world that poetry reveals to us is usually called the common sense world. We do not constitute it in the sense that we create it out of nothing. The world in which we live is there, furthering or impeding our activity, independently of the mind's grasp of it; but as we come to know it, the world is constituted by the means of a symbolic process which is at the heart of the aesthetic activity. What art does is put the world at our disposal (Vivas, p. 74).

Literature gives us a grasp of the world which is in some sense reflected in it (Vivas, p. 110).

Vivas defines the poem and the aesthetic experience as follows:

> A poem is a linguistic artifact, whose function is to organize the primary data of experience that can be exhibited in and through words. With the necessary changes this can be said of all art. Put in different terms, what poetry uniquely does is to reveal a world which is self-sufficient. It does not communicate in the ordinary sense of the term, nor does it imitate or designate existent or imaginary things which can be apprehended independently of the poem. By means of the self-sufficient world that poetry reveals we are able to grasp, as the poem lingers in memory as a redolence, the actual world in which we live. Without the aid of poetry our ambient world remains an inchoate, unstructured chaos (p. 73).

> In order for a poem to function as a self-sufficient whole, we must approach it in an aesthetic attitude. We do so when we read it with rapt, intransitive attention on its full presentational immediacy.... A poem functions as a self-sufficient whole when it has, as we have long known, unity, when its discriminable elements are tied by organic interrelationships in such a manner that our attention is not led off from them but is held captive by them and is fully satisfied in its captivity (p. 76).

Understood in this way, art does not "express" or "imitate." Through the symbolic processes of creation, the artist discovers potential for order and unity in the raw chaos of experience, and he himself does not know the final product until it is accomplished. The audience, of course, is free to espouse or reject his creation as a model, a metaphor, for reality. Joseph Smith was a prophet as revelatory experiences were granted to him; he was a poet as his mortal mind, through the creative process, arrived at the "constitution" of those experiences that is these poems, upon which—for Latter-day Saint believers, of which I emphatically am one—God himself has placed his imprimatur as representations of reality. Any successful work of art provides, during the brief moments when we can fully inhabit it, surcease from the chaos and fragmentation that so much characterize our daily lives and to some extent, lesser or greater, our very selves. Furthermore, it stands as a metaphor for the unity and the orderliness, the meaningful relationship of the part to the whole—the part that each of us is—that human beings yearn to find in the cosmos.

These poems, as works of art that God himself has approved as being his "word," constitute a divine reassurance that the universe is, after all, a unified and orderly place in which every element, every human being, has its meaningful place; that is, all except those who choose to devote the entirety of their very existence to the destruction of that unity; and even they provide a dark background against which the Light shines and so, ironically, take a place in the whole. Everything in the cosmos is a thread in a magnificent fabric that, grasped as a whole (and in some of these poems every human being is offered a final grasp of the whole as God grasps it), is satisfying. For them to work as such a testimony, however, they must be experienced as works of art.

Richard C. Schipp, in "Conceptual Patterns of Repetition in the Doctrine and Covenants and Their Implications," finds theological significance in some of the particular devices employed to achieve the unities that are these poems (and I quote him in concurrence). Schipp observes (p. 157) that (and the italics are all his) "*repetition* of concepts occurred to a high degree" (in the sections that he examined), that "the repetition was *structured* . . . into *patterns* of symmetry," including both "*reverse* repetition" (chiasm) and "*direct* repetition." He further observes: "The patterns gave to the revelations an esthetically pleasing sense of *beauty, symmetry,* and *design.* Each revelation became a 'symphony of words.'" He suggests that the parallelisms were "a means of incorporating a *'built-in system of commentary'* within each revelation," that by them "*context* may be established, *clarifications* may be made, *meanings* may be illuminated, *definitions* may be given," and (p. 158) that "'Punctuation' was inherently incorporated within the revelations through techniques of pattern structuring." He proposes that by these structural patterns the texts "convey eternal symbolism" (p. 149), they "bear record of a higher reality" (p. 150). He proposes that by means of chiasm they are "made to bear record of God as the First and the Last—the Last and The First," and that by them "the

Lord has revealed that the pattern incorporated into all things by the power of His spirit is 'that the first shall be last, and that the last shall be first' in all things" (p. 150).

He further proposes that, in what he called "The Historic Chiasm," "there is an eternal basis for the patterns of reverse repetition which appears in the revelations of the Doctrine and Covenants. That basis is seen in the history (from the beginning to the end) of planet earth and her inhabitants . . . The 'focal point' of 'The Historic Chiasm' was the point at which the earth and mankind began their ascent *back* into the presence of God from whence they have fallen. The 'turning point' of the history of this earth was THE ATONEMENT OF JESUS CHRIST" (pp. 151–52).

Particularly interesting from this point of view is the structural complexity of sections 76 and 1, in which chiasms overlap with chiasms, and chiasms contain chiasms and overlap with and stand in formal relationship to other, nonchiasmic parallel structures, such that any line or word serves as an element of multiple structures. There is thus a structural ambiguity in the text (a type of ambiguity not identified by William Empson in his famous book) that contributes to the total quantum of meaning contained within it. As Shipp observes in his thesis, "Within revelations which come from God, one may discover multiple levels of structuring occurring, that through matching multiple areas, many relationships and levels of patterns may be generated" (p. 16). I would add that these multiple permutations of relationship represent the "both-and" nature of ultimate reality toward which section 93 points.

There is perhaps other meaning in the use of these particular formal devices. They are loose, the control they exert on the shape and development of the composition is gentle, allowing for spontaneity and flexibility, mirroring God's approach to his creation, as he provides a framework in which inferior intelligences may find full development, while respecting their agency and allowing for spontaneity and individual initiative. This is a God who issues commandments, to be sure, but who also says, "It is not meet that I should command in all things; for he that is compelled in all things, the same is a slothful and not a wise servant; wherefore he receiveth no reward. Verily I say, men should be anxiously engaged in a good cause, and do many things of their own free will, and bring to pass much righteousness; for the power is in them, wherein they are agents unto themselves" (D&C 58:26–28). Something approaching free verse seems very suitable to represent the relationship between such a God and such children of God. As a Latter-day Saint hymn puts it, "How gentle God's commands...."

It is likely that the cadence and the parallelistic form of these works reflect the way in which they were received: "line upon line, precept upon precept," thought by thought, the next not given until the previous has been acknowledged and recorded. The parallelism that is so closely related to this kind of rhythm also reflects the principle of "line upon line, precept upon precept." Brigham Young said that "Joseph Smith was a poet" because he caught "the swift thought of God" and revealed it to us (in *The Essential Brigham Young*, p. 241). I do not agree that that is sufficient reason to call Joseph a poet, and not all that I would call poems fit that description, but Joseph's method of composition would seem to indicate that he was capturing "swift thought" as it came to him from somewhere, and it seems rather natural that that thought would fall into a cadenced, incremental, parallelistic form. The formal nature of these texts would seem to suggest that this prosody, this combination of a particular kind of rhythm and a particular kind of parallelism, is in effect the language—or at least a language—of the Spirit.

The thinking of the late Clinton F. Larson bears on this latter point. Larson as poet sought "a transmutation of God and the Holy Ghost into poetry" (in Douglas Airmet, p. 45). He insisted (as I heard him in class lectures) that the transmutation could be achieved only in poetry, and he sought it through a poetic style that he called "Baroque," inspired by Wylie Sypher's *Four Stages of Renaissance Style: Transformation in Art and Literature*. He described in class lectures the following passage from his "Letter from Israel Whiton, 1851" (in *Counterpoint*, pp. 37–41) as an attempt to capture the "feeling of the Spirit" through the "stacking" of clauses in the last sentence to create a syntactical analogue of great height; the sense of of effortless upward movement conveyed by the image of the letter lifting and rising to the cirri; the light of the sun and the image of "the white silver spirit" and the brightness of "golden seal," "white hand," "plumes of cirri," "sunset," "Oquirrh" (with its suggestion of gold); and the sense of enormous space in the sky and the landscape:

> But Eliza is still as I write, and I must only
> Listen. I, Israel Whiton of the Salt Lake Valley,
> Write this letter to you, Mother, from the canyons
> And the butte above my land; it is a leaf

> From the spring before we came, as both you and Eliza
> Know, unanswerable except in the signs that come,
> That I cannot seek. So I give it to the wind
> From the tips of piñons or the butte, and it lifts
> Away, and I try to see it as it diminishes
> Away, then vanishing though I know it is there,
> As you know better than I, Mother . . . And it will rise
> Beyond the golden seal and touch the white hand
> In the cirri plumbing the Oquirrh crest west
> Over the sunset, and it is as if I take a veil
> Full in my hand as I write, as if to let it yield
> To the days consecrated to the journey west
> That holds me aloof from all I have ever known,
> The East and the Cities of my common being,
> As I am here, in Zion, wondering about you
> Who cannot respond except in the barest hints
> Of being that lift over me and show me the way
> To yield and rise into the Kingdom, the sky
> And the land like the white silver spirit
> That we know but is fathomless before us
> and indefinite as the planes of God rising
> Into the sun . . .

That is more regularly metered than Joseph's poems, with its free verse that barely breaks out of blank verse, and it does not employ his parallelism; nevertheless, this from section 88 has something of the "feel" of it, which is also accomplished partly by a combination of cadence and images of light:

> The earth rolls upon her wings,
> and the sun giveth his light by day,
> and the moon giveth her light by night,
> and the stars also give their light,
> as they roll upon their wings in their glory,
> in the midst of the power of God.

As a matter of fact, almost all of the selections from the "works of Joseph Smith" that have been canonized, outside the Book of Mormon, exhibit a use of cadence and parallelism that give them a "poetic" quality. Joseph seems to have arrived at a solution very like Larson's for the same problem. The contrast between words that are canonized and words that are not is particularly striking in the original manuscript from which the pieces of Doctrine and Covenants 121:1–25, 122:1–9 are drawn. There is thus evidence for Larson's claim that what Joseph Smith experienced as "the Spirit" is best represented by poetry.

If poems like Joseph's represent "the swift thought of God," then the converse seems plausible: the form of these poems suggests that submission to this kind of poetry helps to prepare the reader also to capture that "swift thought" in replication of the very experience that gave rise to the poetry in the first place. The texts are thus designed to serve as catalysts of revelatory experience. The intransitive character of these texts, as not merely "poetry" but also as unified poems, contributes to that purpose by keeping the attention of the reader focused within them, as peering through a verbal lens—a verbal seerstone—toward the reality that lies beyond them. Section 93, after all, contains this remarkable promise, which is contained in much the same words in other places:

> It shall come to pass that every soul
> > who forsaketh his sins
> > and cometh unto me
> > and calleth on my name
> > and obeyeth my voice
> > and keepeth my commandments
> shall see my face
> > and know that I am

The reader is invited, not only to contemplate the truths spoken of in the poem, but to see and know for himself, and the poem is so constructed as to assist him toward obtaining those experiences. Though the poem has extraliterary intent, in order fully to realize that intent it must be read in a literary way; it is necessary to pay close attention to the "words on the page," not only in their transitive, referential nature, but also in how they work together intransitively, relate to each other, condition each other, as parts of the aesthetically unified whole. The intransitive quality of the structure, its power to hold the reader with the poem itself, serves to concentrate the mind, as on—through—a seerstone. That seems particularly true of Doctrine and Covenants 76, in which the center of a great chiasm focuses the mind on a capitulation of the degrees of glory. These poems thus are designed to be transformational in nature, to have the power to change men and their world not only indirectly, by the communication of meaning, but more directly, by their action upon men, as an operation of sanctifying grace.

These poems belong in the biblical tradition. They derive much of their meaning from their position within that tradition. If the Book of Mormon is the "keystone" of the religion of the Latter-day Saints, the King James Version of the Bible (KJV) remains as its scriptural foundation, and it is also the foundation of the literary edifice that is the "works of Joseph Smith." One way in which this relationship functions is in Joseph's frequent use of biblical language, but with a twist: although the Bible is the foundation upon which Joseph builds his literary edifice, it is not the standard KJV that serves so, but rather Joseph's "revisioning" of the KJV. Joseph was *mythopoietes*, "maker of myth"—myth, not in the sense of a story that is not true, but in the sense of a story that unfolds a worldview. These short poems *mean* in relation to that great story, the most complete account of which is the Bible, but a Bible remade by a great act of *mythopoeia*, a Bible "revisioned." Exploration of this thesis—of Joseph as *mythopoietes*— lies beyond the scope of this little essay on a handful of poems, but it resides in the background of this commentary.

Joseph as poet also fits in the the nineteenth century (defined as a "long" century that began in 1789 and ended in 1914). In a discussion of section 88, Richard L. Bushman says that "nothing in nineteenth-century literature resembles it" (p. 206), and presumably he would say the same of the other sections treated here. That seems to be an overstatement.

I have already argued in the commentary on section 93 that philosophically the text exhibits affinities with certain post-Kantian thinkers, including the American Transcendentalists that were Joseph's countrymen and near contemporaries. Also notable is a stylistic similarity between Joseph and Coleridge. Coleridge is regarded as the inventor of "conversational" verse, as exemplified by these lines from "Frost at Midnight":

> Therefore all seasons shall be sweet to thee,
> Whether the summer clothe the general earth
> With greenness, or the redbreast sit and sing
> Betwixt the tufts of snow on the bare branch
> Of mossy apple-tree, while the night thatch

> Smokes in the sun-thaw; whether the eave-drops fall
> Heard only in the trances of the blast,
> Or if the secret ministry of frost
> Shall hang them up in silent icicles,
> Quietly shining to the quiet Moon.

This quiet, pensive, conversational mood, achieved by Coleridge through unrhymed iambic pentameter, is achieved in section 88:45, already cited above in connection with another matter, through unrhymed, unmetered though cadenced parallelism and a similar imagery. Also notable is a similarity in structure between "Frost at Midnight" and section 93. In both, the speaker speaks first in first and third person, and then abruptly shifts to second person. The analogy is not exact, but it is close. Compare this transition in "Frost at Midnight"

> . . . and I snatched
> A hasty glance, and still my heart leaped up,
> For still I hoped to see the *stranger's* face,
> Townsman, or aunt, or sister more beloved,
> My play-mate when we both were clothed alike!
> Dear Babe, that sleepest cradled by my side,
> Whose gentle breathings, heard in this deep calm. . . .

with this in section 93:

> and that wicked one cometh and taketh away light and truth,
> through disobedience,
> from the children of men,
> and because of the tradition of their fathers.
> But I have commanded you
> to bring up your children in light and truth;

Moreover, "Frost at Midnight" employs the word "but" to make another transition similar to the one above from section 93:

> . . . For I was reared
> In the great city, pent 'mid cloisters dim,
> And saw nought lovely but the sky and stars.
> But thou, my babe! shalt wander like a breeze
> By lakes and sandy shores. . . .

Moreover, the nineteenth century has two other great visionary poets, William Blake (1757–1827) and Arthur Rimbaud (1854–1891). Compare the aphoristic style and the cadence of 93:21–26 and 33–36 and the syntactical parallelism that is evidenced all over these six poems with those of this this selection from Blake's "The Marriage of Heaven and Hell":

> The pride of the peacock is the glory of God.
> The lust of the goat is the bounty of God.
> The wrath of the lion is the wisdom of God.
> The nakedness of woman is the work of God.
> Excess of sorrow laughs. Excess of joy weeps.
> The roaring of lions, the howling of wolves, the raging of the stormy sea, and the destructive sword, are portions of eternity, too great for the eye of man.

Compare the enumerations and the cadence of 93:1–3 with those of this from Rimbaud's *Alchemy of the Word* (as translated by Wallace Fowlie):

> I like stupid paintings, door panels, stage sets, back-drops for acrobats, signs popular engravings, old-fashioned literature, church Latin, erotic books with bad spelling, novels of our grandmothers, fairy tales, little books from childhood, old operas, ridiculous refrains, naïve rhythms.
> I dreamed of crusades, of unrecorded voyages of discovery, of republics with no history, of hushed-up religious wars, revolutions in customs, displacements of races and continents: I believed in every kind of witchcraft.

The content of their visions was in major respects different from Joseph's (though it would be interesting to explore parallels), and a believer in Joseph's visions will insist that they were of a different kind from those others, but the point to be made here is that Joseph was not alone in the nineteenth century as a visionary poet, and he resembles them in prosody and style, as he does also another kind of poet, Walt Whitman (1819–1892), who has already been mentioned in this essay. Parallelisms of Joseph bear comparison with series such as this from Whitman, in "When Lilacs last in the Dooryard Bloomed"—to be compared with the series of "if" clauses in D&C 122:

> Coffin that passes through lanes and streets,
> Through day and night with the great cloud darkening the land,
> With the show of the States themselves as of crape-veil'd women standing,
> With the pomp of the inloop'd flags with the cities draped in black,
> With the show of the States themselves as of crape-veil'd women standing,
> With processions long and winding and the flambeaus of the night,
> With the countless torches lit, with the silent seas of faces and the unbared heads,
> With the waiting depot, the arriving coffin, and the sombre faces,
> With dirges through the night, with the thousand voices rising strong and solemn,
> With all the mournful voices of the dirges pour'd around the coffin,

Compare the relaxed rhythm of 93:40–53 with this from Whitman's *Song of Myself*:

> I saw the marriage of the trapper in the open air in the far west, the bride was a red girl,
> Her father and his friends sat near cross-legged and dumbly smoking,
>   they had moccasins to their feet and large thick blankets hanging from their shoulders.
> On a bank lounged the trapper, he was drest mostly in skins,
>   his luxuriant beard and curls protected his neck,
>   he held his bride by the hand.
> She had long eyelashes, her head was bare,
>   her coarse straight locks descended upon her voluptuous limbs and reach'd to her feet.

Joseph's use of biblical language finds parallel in the fiction of Herman Melville, who comes later in the chronology of American literature. For example (drawn from a novel full of possible ones), the first line of section 1 places the poem squarely in the biblical tradition and raises certain expectations; the first line of Melville's *Moby Dick* does the same: "Call me Ishmael." Melville's narrator is thus identified with the alienated, unhappy character of Genesis who goes by the same name, as the voice of, say, section 93 is identified with the oracular voices of the Bible.

Joseph also anticipates in his poems the French Symbolists of the later nineteenth and early twentieth centuries. "French Romantic poetry projected subjective emotions, sometimes with great strength and beauty, but by and large its lyricism remained declamatory and oratorical in nature," Elaine Marks notes in her introduction to *French Poetry from Baudelaire to the Present* (p. 12). These poems of Joseph also are "declamatory and oratorical in nature," but there is something much deeper in them. Marks further notes, speaking of the French poets who succeeded the French Romantics:

> All the great poets of the second half of the nineteenth century had extra-literary intentions: that is, they sought to infuse suggestions of transcendent power and meaning into their art. Baudelaire's search for the Ideal, Rimbaud's quest for the 'future vigueur' that would transform men, Mallarmé's for the words that would mime the order of the universe, underline the metaphysical-religious objective of their poetry. For these poets, and for their followers, secondary writers who called themselves Symbolists, the artist's role became that of a sort of high priest, if not a god, whose artistic creations take on a kind of sacred character.

Joseph, whose poems are offered as metaphors for eternal realities, was a poet of that sort; Latter-day Saints, at least, can recognize him as a poet-priest. Marks recognizes that "one need not accept their [the Symbolists'] theories as gospel, to be sure," and many, even most, will not accept the revelations to Joseph Smith as gospel; but something like what Marks went on to say of the Symbolists might also be said of Joseph: "The promethean aims that were an integral part of the Symbolist credo help illuminate certain aspects of these works. Whether or not the poets achieved or attained what they hoped to through the creative act, they left behind many exceptionally fine poems, a number of them great" (pp. 13–14).

As seen through the lens of faith of a Latter-day Saint, however, Joseph is not merely an anticipator of others or an also-ran. Rather, the "poetic achievement" of Joseph Smith (in its totality, not only in these few texts) *is* the main current of nineteenth-century American literature, indeed of world literature, from its beginning to its imminent end. The others are the also-rans. Emerson is Joseph Smith Lite. It might well be that the "problem of belief" posed by these poems of Joseph Smith is insuperable, that nonbelievers might be unable to achieve the aesthetic distance necessary for them to appreciate these compositions as poems, or unable to separate out from the bones of doctrines they reject enough metaphorical meat to give them the satisfactions they seek in poetry. Nevertheless, though readers outside the faith have some excuse for not taking Joseph Smith seriously as a poet, the Latter-day Saints have none.

Works Cited

Airmet, Douglas E. "Mormon Poets Talk about Their Craft." *The New Era.* 5:8 (Aug. 1975): 44–49. Print.
Alter, Robert. *The Art of Biblical Poetry.* New York: Basic Books, 1985.
Brooks, Cleanth. *The Well Wrought Urn: Studies in the Structure of Poetry.* New York, London: Harcourt Brace Jovanovich, 1975.
Bushman, Richard Lyman. *Joseph Smith: Rough Stone Rolling.* New York: Alfred A. Knopf, 2005.
Ciardi, John. *How Does a Poem Mean? Part Three of An Introduction to Literature.* Cambridge, Mass.: The Riverside Press, 1959.
Coleridge, Samuel Taylor. *Biographia Literaria.* 2 vols. Ed. J. Shawcross. London: Oxford University Press, 1954.
Emerson, Ralph Waldo. *Essays: First and Second Series.* Library of American Paperback Classics, 1991.
Gorton, H. Clay. *Language of the Lord.* Bountiful, Ut.: Horizon Publishers, 1993.
Harper, Steven C. *Making Sense of the Doctrine and Covenants: A Guided Tour through Modern Revelations.* Salt Lake City: Deseret Book, 2008.
Larson, Clinton F. *Counterpoint: A Book of Poems.* Provo: Brigham Young University Press, 1973.
Langer, Susanne K. *Philosophy in a New Key: A Study in the Symbolism of Reason, Rite, and Art.* 3rd ed. Cambridge, Mass.: Harvard University Press, 1957.
King, Charles Francis. *The Doctrine & Covenants Completely Restructured (Including Chiasm).* 2d ed., rev. Charles Francis King, 2000.
Marks, Elaine. *French Poetry from Baudelaire to the Present.* New York: Dell, 1962.
McMurrin, Sterling M. *The Theological Foundations of the Mormon Religion and The Philosophical Foundations of Mormon Theology.* Salt Lake City: Signature Books, 2000.
Peterson, Roger K. Joseph Smith Prophet–Poet: A Literary Analysis of Writings Commonly Associated with His Name. Doctoral dissertation, The Brigham Young University, 1981.
Pound, Ezra. *Make It New: Essays.* London: Faber and Faber, 1935.
———. *The Spirit of Romance.* New York: New Directions Books, 1952.
Pratt, Parley P. *The Autobiography of Parley P. Pratt.* Edited by Parley P. Pratt Jr. New York: Russell Brothers, 1874.
Schopenhauer, Arthur. *The World as Will and Representation.* Vol. I. Trans. E. F. J. Payne. New York: Dover Publications, 1969.

Seshachari, Candadai. "Revelation: The Cohesive Element in International Mormonism." *Dialogue: A Journal of Mormon Thought.* XIII.4 (Winter 1980). 38–46.

Shipp, Richard C. Conceptual Patterns of Repetition in the Doctrine and Covenants and Their Implications. Master's thesis, The Brigham Young University, 1975.

Smith, Barbara Herrnstein. *Poetic Closure: A Study of How Poems End.* Chicago, London: The University of Chicago Press, 1968.

Smith, Joseph. *Personal Writings of Joseph Smith.* Rev. ed. Comp. and ed. Dean C. Jessee. Salt Lake City: Deseret Book, 2002.

———. *Teachings of the Prophet Joseph Smith.* Sel. and arr. Joseph Fielding Smith. Salt Lake City: Deseret Book, 1976.

———. *The Joseph Smith Papers, Revelations and Translations, Volume 1: Manuscript Revelation Books.* Ed. Robin Scott Jensen, et. al. Salt Lake City: The Church Historian's Press, 2011.

Sypher, Wylie. *Four Stages of Renaissance Style: Transformations in Art and Literature 1400–1700.* Garden City, New York: Doubleday, 1955.

Vivas, Eliseo. *Creation and Discovery: Essays in Criticism and Aesthetics.* New York: The Noonday Press, 1955.

Whitney, Orson F. *The Poetical Writings of Orson F. Whitney: Poems and Poetic Prose.* Salt Lake City: Juvenile Instructor Office, 1889.

Widtsoe, John A. *Rational Theology as Taught by The Church of Jesus Christ of Latter-day Saints.* Salt Lake City: General Priesthood Committee, 1915.

Young, Brigham. *The Essential Brigham Young.* Salt Lake City: Signature Books, 1992.

About the Author

Colin Blaine Douglas was born in 1944 and brought up in Western Washington; is an enrolled member of the Samish Indian Nation; became a Latter-day Saint at the age of sixteen; served in the Brazilian Mission in 1964–1966; served in Military Intelligence in the Regular Army and the Utah National Guard, retiring as a sergeant first class; attended the University of Washington as a journalism major and received a bachelor's degree in psychology and a master's degree in American literature at Brigham Young University; was employed for twenty years as an editor in the Curriculum Department of The Church of Jesus Christ of Latter-day Saints; edited and reported for the *Magna* (Utah) *Times* newspaper for two years; with the former Linda Jean Wells, to whom he was married in 1969, is the father of seven; has resided in Utah since 1971; as literary favorites names Latter-day Saint scripture (including the Bible), Arthur Rimbaud, André Breton, Ezra Pound, T. S. Eliot, Kenneth Rexroth, Gary Snyder, and Philip Lamantia.

www.ingramcontent.com/pod-product-compliance
Lightning Source LLC
Chambersburg PA
CBHW032126090426
42743CB00007B/487